THE RED FOX OF COLDITZ

THE RED FOX OF COLDITZ

Lieutenant AM Sinclair DSO

VERE HAYES

Pen & Sword
MILITARY
AN IMPRINT OF PEN & SWORD BOOKS LTD.
YORKSHIRE – PHILADELPHIA

First published in Great Britain in 2026 by
PEN AND SWORD MILITARY
An imprint of
Pen & Sword Books Limited
Yorkshire – Philadelphia

Print ISBN 978 1 03610 989 9
ePUB ISBN 978 1 03610 991 2
ePDF ISBN 978 1 03610 993 6

A CIP catalogue record for this book is available from the British Library.

Typeset in Times New Roman 12/16 by
SJmagic DESIGN SERVICES, India.
Printed and bound in the UK by CPI Group (UK) Ltd.

The Publisher's authorised representative in the EU for product safety is Authorised Rep Compliance Ltd., Ground Floor, 71 Lower Baggot Street,
Dublin D02 P593, Ireland.
www.arccompliance.com

For a complete list of Pen & Sword titles please contact
PEN & SWORD BOOKS LIMITED
George House, Units 12 & 13, Beevor Street, Off Pontefract Road,
Barnsley, South Yorkshire, S71 1HN, England
E-mail: enquiries@pen-and-sword.co.uk
Website: www.pen-and-sword.co.uk

or

PEN AND SWORD BOOKS
1950 Lawrence Rd, Havertown, PA 19083, USA
E-mail: uspen-and-sword@casematepublishers.com
Website: www.penandswordbooks.com

CONTENTS

THE RED FOX

LIEUTENANT MA SINCLAIR DSO, KRRC 1918 – 1944

Albert Michael Sinclair, 'Mike' to his Regimental friends and referred to as 'Mike' from here onwards, was born on 26 February 1918 in Kensington, London; the middle of three sons born to Colonel Thomas Charles Sinclair, CBE and Iris Lucy Sinclair, née Lund. The Sinclairs were a military family and all three sons followed their father into the Army.

Mike's elder brother, Christopher, was commissioned into the Rifle Brigade (RB) in 1937 and served with 2RB in India. Shortly before the outbreak of war the Battalion moved to Palestine to train as a Motor Battalion and then to Egypt where it joined the newly formed 7th Armoured Division; he was awarded an MC and Bar in 1941 while serving in the Western Desert. Mike's younger brother John was killed at Anzio in 1944 serving with the Scots Guards. Mike was commissioned into the Kings Royal Rifle Corps (KRRC, often referred to as *the 60th*) in 1939. I had been told that each of the three sons had given their mother, Lady Sinclair, a brooch in the form of their regimental cap badge but I found that this was not so; Iris Sinclair was not 'Lady Sinclair' as I had been led to believe but simply Mrs Sinclair, the wife of Colonel Thomas Sinclair; none of her sons had given her a brooch in the form of their regimental badge and Mike was never known in the family as 'Mike', to them he was always Michael.

The truth is that Iris Sinclair was distraught at the death of Mike so soon after her youngest son John had been killed in action at Anzio. Christopher Sinclair, with whom I was in contact, wrote in 1984: 'My father had bought the 60th brooch as a memento for my mother after Michael's death. It was both her wish and mine that after her death someone in the Regiment should have it.' Shortly after she died, Christopher Sinclair contacted the Celer et Audax Club, the 60th Officers Club, to express her wish concerning the brooch and the matter was passed to the Royal Green Jackets Regimental Secretary. With the reduction in the size of the army since 1945 many regiments had been amalgamated, among them the KRRC, that had been one of the forming regiments of The Royal Green Jackets. I was the last Officer Cadet who, in December 1965, had been accepted for a Regular Commission into what was then 2nd Battalion The Green Jackets (Kings Royal Rifle Corps) before it became 2nd Battalion The Royal Green Jackets (2RGJ) on 1 January 1966.

Just over ten years later, in 1976, I was serving with 3 RGJ in Berlin having just got married. I was asked by Colonel Ian McCausland, the Regimental Secretary and formerly an officer in the KRRC, if my wife Penny and I would like to have the brooch that was in the form of a 60th cap badge; it was a Maltese Cross of platinum and gold set with diamonds surmounted by a King's Crown; we accepted with delight and thanks. Thus began my interest in Mike Sinclair, known to the German guards at Colditz as *'der Rote Fuchs'*, (the Red Fox), who had spent more time 'free' in occupied Europe than any other escapee, but who had never made a home run.

The brooch was sent to us and over the years a series of remarkable coincidences followed. We found that the West Berlin Commonwealth War Graves Commission Cemetery had been established in 1945 as a central burial ground for aircrew and prisoners of war who were interred in the Berlin area and further afield, in what was then East Germany. Colditz Castle was in East Germany, so Mike's body had been moved to Berlin. Coincidences continued:

- The son of Mike's close friend Grismond (Gris) Davies-Scourfield was an officer in the Royal Green Jackets and we served together in Germany.
- When I was an instructor at The Staff College, Camberley, I asked the French Liaison officer if he would translate for me a letter I had received from Charles Klein, a French Officer who had escaped from Colditz with Mike. He agreed and having glanced at the letter exclaimed; 'this is remarkable, I have heard much about this officer, he was a boyfriend of my mother!'
- Tom Hamilton-Baillie, whose father Jock had been in Colditz with Mike, was an officer in 2 RGJ. I served with Tom on several occasions and met his father.
- When I was commanding a Brigade my Deputy Brigade Commander was a Territorial Officer, Colonel Piers Storie-Pugh, whose father had been a POW in Colditz with Mike.

I collected a great deal of material about Mike and Colditz over the years and it is to my shame that it has taken me so long to write the story of a remarkable man whose many escapes remain largely untold or have been misrepresented. In the 1955 film *The Colditz Story*, Mike's most audacious escape attempt involving the impersonation of the German Guard Commander nicknamed 'Franz Joseph', to whom Mike, with his red hair, bore a remarkable resemblance, is attributed to the Senior British Officer in Colditz played by Eric Portman. Mike's last attempt (on which he lost his life), although portrayed accurately, is attributed in the film to 'Mac McGill', a fictitious fellow British prisoner played by Christopher Rhodes, later Sir Christopher George, Rhodes 3rd Baronet, who served with the Essex Regiment in the Second World War, reaching the rank of Lieutenant-Colonel and winning a Croix de Guerre and United States Legion of Merit.

Mike, like his elder brother Christopher, was educated at Winchester College where, to quote his brother: 'he did well at work and play, always very sturdy and unafraid'. He was an accomplished left-hand bowler in the cricket XI and an above average golfer, close to winning a Blue at Cambridge where he had gone on to read modern languages, specifically French and German, in both of which he became fluent and gained a First Class Honours Degree. Redheaded, stocky, and with a strong sense of duty and great determination, he was commissioned into the KRRC in July 1939, joining 2 KRRC – one of the two mechanised infantry battalions known officially as Motor Battalions, in 1st Armoured Division.

The story of his part in the defence of Calais in 1940, his capture when the city fell and the escapes he made thereafter – none of which, sadly, resulted in a home run, and in the last of which in late 1944 he lost his life – are the substance of this short account. It is a story that has never before been told fully; indeed, as already described, his most audacious attempt and his death have been misrepresented. Mike was always determined to escape and return to active service, he saw it as his duty. Think back to being 22 years old, and from there think forward to being 26; an awful lot seems to happen in those five years, and it is this period of life that this story of Mike Sinclair covers, five years of captivity and frustration despite his unceasing quest for freedom.

The supplement to the *London Gazette* of 29 August 1946 records the award of The Distinguished Service Order (DSO) to Lieutenant Albert Michael Sinclair (75265); the citation for the award written by Major General VM Fortune reads:

> From the moment he was taken prisoner at CALAIS in 1940 until he was shot in attempting to escape in daylight on 25 Sep 1944, Lt Sinclair devoted the whole of his energies to the task of escaping and so returning to continue the fight. He never deviated from this set purpose and, in spite of setbacks and the hardest of luck, his courage and determination never wavered.

In all he made no fewer than seven great attempts to escape, each one having been planned to the smallest detail, entailing months of preparation and careful calculation. Even after being wounded in September 1943, during one of these magnificent efforts, he never gave up but began to prepare for his next attempt almost before he had recovered from his wound. On four separate occasions he was successful in getting out of the camp – a most difficult and hazardous undertaking from Oflag IVC, which was a 'Straflager' for persistent escapers – and he spent more months of freedom in GERMANY and other occupied European countries than any other Prisoner of War. On each of these four occasions, when complete freedom seemed to be within his grasp, he was dogged by just that bit of bad luck that turned the scales against him.

The benefit of his experience was always available to any fellow prisoner of war wishing to escape and many successful escapers have testified to the great help he gave them in their planning. No less than fourteen Senior Officers (including Gen. Fortune) have recorded in their official reports that Lt Sinclair was the most outstanding escaper they had known. His sustained gallantry and courage, his never-failing enthusiasm and his steadfastness of purpose were an inspiration to all.

The citation has a handwritten addendum by Major General V.M. Fortune, GOC 51st Highland Division, who was taken prisoner at St Valery-en-Caux after the surrender of the Division on 12 June 1940, when naval evacuation proved impossible and supplies of ammunition had been exhausted. Major General Fortune spent the rest of the war as the most senior British officer in captivity; as such he worked to improve the conditions of the men under his command and, even after suffering a stroke in 1944, refused repatriation. He was finally liberated in April 1945 and made KBE. Just over a year later he added the following, in his own hand, below the typewritten citation for the award of the DSO to Michael Sinclair:

> I was at VIIc with Lt Sinclair and afterwards at Fort VIII Posen from which he escaped in 1941. I had, before I heard of Lt Sinclair's death at Colditz, decided that I would recommend him for a DSO for his previous many gallant escapes but as a POW I was not able to take action till I was released in March 1945.
>
> V.M. Fortune
> Major General
> June 16, 1946

In 1985, I wrote to the *British Army Review* to dispute an assertion by Sir Martin Lindsay, Bt, in the August 1980 edition, in which he had written that 'one rule governing the award of the DSO was that it should not be given to a POW', and 'that only one exception was on record, Major T.A.G. Pritchard RWF'. He was wrong, arguably on both counts, but sadly he had died four years earlier and I was unable to correspond with him. However, for the record, Major Pritchard won his DSO for his involvement in the destruction of the Brindisi aqueduct in Italy and not for any actions while a POW. As for the award to Mike, the DSO was instituted by Queen Victoria in 1886 to reward individual instances of Meritorious or Distinguished Service in war that were deemed just short of deserving the Victoria Cross (VC). In 1944, it was a decoration for officers only, typically major or higher, with separate awards to lower ranks and it was normally given for service under fire, or conditions equivalent to service in actual combat, but as there was never a 'rule' that debarred the award of a DSO to a POW, the award to Mike could not break it. As was noted in a Loose Minute on the subject, sent from a staff officer in the Ministry of Defence to the Military Secretary: 'While it may be considered 'hair splitting' the decision was clearly in good faith and did not break the posthumous rule – rather, it skilfully evaded it to ensure justice was done to the memory of a very brave officer.'

CHAPTER 2

THE DEFENCE AND CAPTURE OF CALAIS

MAY 1940

In April 1939, when the German invasion of Czechoslovakia and the Italian invasion of Albania presaged another war, two Green Jacket Regular Battalions, 2 KRRC and 1 RB, were the Motor Battalions in the Support Group of 1st Armoured Division, and the only mechanised all arms formation in the British Army at that time. They were mobile infantry trained to operate in close support of armour, ready to restore momentum should built up areas or unsuitable country be encountered and need clearing; they drove everywhere, each rifle section having its own vehicle able to carry men, bedding, food and cooking equipment, keep up with the armour, and operate independently. This was a role that suited Green Jackets and their traditional independence of action away from infantry of the line but sadly they were never to fight as Motor Battalions; as is recorded in *Famous Regiments: The Rifle Brigade*, and is equally applicable to the KRRC: 'It was a tragedy that those who had evolved and perfected the principles on which a motor battalion would operate were to be destroyed [at Calais] before having the opportunity to act on them.'

Both battalions maintained their reputation for marksmanship and were acknowledged as coming from the best shooting regiments in the Army, winning trophies each year in the annual Army and Inter

Services competitions at Bisley. Their skill at arms would prove invaluable in the forthcoming battle.

On being commissioned in 1939, Mike joined 2 KRRC as a platoon commander and was put in command of 'A' Company Scout Platoon. 1st Armoured Division was not fully equipped at the outbreak of war and did not deploy to France with the British Expeditionary Force (BEF) in autumn 1939, moving instead to billets in Stalbridge, Dorset, where they were to be based throughout the 'Phoney War' until the German surprise attack through the Ardennes in May 1940, threatened to cut off the BEF from the Channel ports and evacuation to England. Over the autumn the focus for 2 KRRC and 1 RB was on infantry training; little combined arms exercising was possible as the armoured Regiments were being re-equipped. This training was interrupted early in November when intelligence sources warned of possible German landings in East Anglia and the Battalion was deployed at short notice to Braintree in Essex to meet any invasion; they remained there over Christmas before returning to Stalbridge. One of the tasks given to the Battalion, once back, was to train reservists who had been called up, and it was on this duty that Mike was deployed in May 1940 when the news reached him that 2 KRRC was to be sent to France. This prompted him to return immediately to the Battalion and resume command of 'A' Company Scout Platoon.

Each rifle company in the Battalion had one of these scout platoons equipped with Universal Carriers, better known today as Bren Gun Carriers; there were three sections of three Universal Carriers each in these platoons with two further carriers and five motorcycles in the platoon HQ of an officer and fourteen riflemen. Each section carrier had a three-man crew of a non-commissioned officer (NCO), a rifleman and a driver-mechanic. One carrier in each section was commanded by a sergeant, the other two by corporals; all the carriers were armed with a Bren guns and one in each section also had a Boyes Anti-Tank Rifle, a bolt action weapon, firing 0.55inch armour-piercing rounds effective against light armour. Although the crews were normally exposed while travelling, if they came under enemy fire, they could pull a lever to lower the front seat so the gunner and driver were below the level of the front bullet proof screen while the third man could crouch behind his own bullet proof screen in the rear of the carrier. This was the organisation of the platoon that Mike commanded in 'A' Company and was to lead into action at Calais.

Following the German invasion of Norway in April 1940, a new brigade in the British order of battle, 30 Infantry Brigade, commanded by Brigadier Claude Nicholson, had been formed in the expectation of a call for reinforcements to be deployed there; the principal units earmarked for the brigade were 2 KRRC, 1 RB and 1 QVR (Queen Victoria's Rifles), until 1939 a Territorial Army (TA) unit, and now a lightly armed Motorcycle Battalion of 550 all ranks, equipped with motor cycles and motor cycle/side car combinations; their weapons included a small number of Bren guns, Boyes anti-tank rifles and 2-inch mortars; around a third of the Battalion were drivers and being classed as cavalry were armed with revolvers only. The Brigade did not deploy to Norway as had been expected but nevertheless retained under command the units that had been assigned to it and remained a deployable formation. Around 1pm in the morning of 10 May, following the unanticipated German offensive through the Ardennes that bypassed the Maginot Line and broke through into northern France, an order for 2 KRRC to be ready to move at first light with war loads was received, triggering frenetic activity; all thought that they were destined to join the BEF. For the Scout Platoons loading up their carriers in pitch darkness, and in short time, was far from easy but had been practised many times and everything had its place – Bren guns, rifles, tripods, ammunition, grenades, camouflage nets, rations, water cans, tools, maps, concertina wire, tarpaulin, personal kit and anti-gas equipment. Thanks to the practise loading that had been done they were ready to move with a little time in hand – quickly taken up by the Riflemen saying tearful farewells to their local girlfriends. They were not, however, heading for France.

Concern about a possible landing, perhaps an invasion, had prompted the order to deploy to Essex but directions to prepare to repel the anticipated landing were quickly rescinded and the Battalion was withdrawn to Bury St Edmunds. Unexpectedly, they were able to relax there for a number of days, swimming and sunbathing in the sunny weather. For most of them it would be the last time they would enjoy anything similar for five years.

On 12 May, the German attack into Holland and Belgium which the Allies had been anticipating saw the implementation of the plan to establish defensive positions on the line of the Dyle River. The simultaneous German advance through the Ardennes and crossing of the Meuse on 13 May was unexpected since the area was assessed not as impassable, but certainly unsuitable for an armoured advance. With the bulk of the Allied forces deployed in Belgium there was little to stop the Germans as they sliced across the Allied supply lines, dislocating their command and control. It seemed likely that German forces would soon reach the coast, cutting off and isolating the BEF, but a combined French and British counterattack into their flank at Arras showed how potentially exposed they were. By 20 May, German spearheads had reached Abbeville and swung north to cut off the BEF from the Channel coast. However, four days later on 24 May, fearful of their vulnerability, Hitler ordered the Panzer columns advancing towards St Omer and Boulogne to halt, and the Luftwaffe to neutralise Calais until the marching German infantry divisions arrived to assault and capture the port.

On 19 May Lieutenant-General Brownrigg, the Adjutant General of the BEF, had appointed Colonel Holland, a Staff Officer in the BEF Rear HQ in Boulogne, to take command of the British troops in Calais and arrange the evacuation of non-combatant personnel, 'useless mouths' as he described them, along with the wounded. When Colonel Holland arrived he found no plans had been made to defend the port or to evacuate the non-teeth arm personnel and RAF ground crews who were arriving there in a steady stream; he therefore set up a transit camp where they could await movement to England, and used the ships and ferries on which 30 Brigade was arriving to evacuate them, and the wounded, to Dover. On 21 May The destroyer *HMS Venomous* picked up some 200 civilians of the long-established British community in Calais, along with personnel and secret equipment from the 'loop station' at Sangatte a few miles west of Calais. This was where the current produced by submarines passing over loops of cable lying on the seabed between Sangatte and St Margaret's Bay, close to Dover, could be detected, enabling mines to be detonated, or destroyers and anti-submarine trawlers alerted, to intercept U-Boats entering the Atlantic via the English Channel.

In England, on Tuesday 21 May, orders came through that 2 KRRC was to move 'at once' to Southampton and embark for France. The news of the German offensive was sombre, it looked as if this was, at last, the real thing and they would soon be in action. The Battalion moved off in two columns, wheeled and tracked, the latter consisting of the Scout Platoons. 'A' Company Scout Platoon commanded by Mike led the way as the senior among them, with 'B' Company Gris Davies-Scourfield, 'C' Company Phil Pardoe and 'D' Company Dick Warre following, 20 yards between vehicles, 200 yards between sections/platoons, and stopping every two hours for a short rest. They drove without lights which slowed progress and it began to rain, gently at first then steadily getting heavier, soaking everyone and everything. Halting in the early hours to fill up they were given most welcome cups of tea by the locals before continuing their journey reaching Hertford Bridge Flats in Surrey around 10.30 and pausing again to enjoy an even more welcome breakfast. The rain stopped and they soon dried out as they drove on, arriving, very tired, in Southampton in the early afternoon of 22 May. On arrival they were met by staff Officers who collected their maps and had them remove any personal kit from their vehicles before sending them with the drivers to be loaded onto the ships that were to take them across the Channel to France; the rest of the Battalion was sent off to a rest camp for a wash and hot meal. Feeling responsible for his drivers Gris stayed with them and by chance, as loading was nearly complete, met a WO2 wearing KRRC uniform, who wished him luck and remarked that in his opinion 'the Regiment was going the wrong way', hardly a reassuring point of view! Meanwhile the rest of the Battalion had formed up in full equipment to march to the docks for embarkation; a roll call was taken and the Battalion set off amid cheering crowds to board *SS Royal Daffodil*, along with HQ 30 Brigade. They sailed at 11 am on Thursday 23 May.

1 QVR and 3 RTR had sailed the previous day and were already in Calais. In the chaos and confusion of the situation unfolding in France, staff officers at The War Office in London, mistakenly believing that 1 QVR manpower was a third more than its true established strength, and with limited space on the available shipping, ordered them to move at short notice and leave their transport behind. It was a staff error that deprived them of their mobility and all technical means of communication; as Lieutenant Colonel Ellison-Macartney, their Commanding Officer, was to write later: 'The Battalion left for Calais shorn of its mobility and communications; it fought in a role divorced from its training and practice, it dived straight into battle.' 1 QVR disembarked in Calais at midday on 22 May without their motorcycles, transport or 3-inch mortars, and with only smoke bombs for the 2-inch mortars; the drivers were armed with revolvers for which they each had only six rounds and wisely scavenged for rifles and ammunition among the equipment dumped on the quay by those hastily departing for England. Their orders were to take necessary steps to secure the town pending the arrival of 30 Brigade, further evidence of the staff misunderstanding of their role and capability.

Now turning his attention to the task of securing the port, Colonel Holland was astonished to find as 1 QVR disembarked, that a motorcycle battalion had been ordered to leave all of its vehicles, including motorcycles, in England; nevertheless, he ordered them to deploy and block six key roads leading to the port from the south and south west, an enormous perimeter of several miles for less than 600 men with no transport to cover. These roads were congested with a chaotic and bewildered mix of British, French and Belgian troops, from formations and units thrown into disarray by the speed of the German advance. With their chains of command dislocated they were now pouring into the port in a continuous stream, in vehicles or walking mingled with refugees and often six abreast. Moving off on foot 1 QVR, despite the chaos on the roads, completed their deployments in accordance with their orders by late evening 22 May.

Like 1 QVR, 3 RTR based in Fordington near Southampton had been ordered to move at short notice, receiving orders at 8 pm on 21 May to entrain two-and-a-half hours later. Although they were at four hours' notice to move with most of the soldiers on a pass until midnight, all but ten men and one officer were collected in the time given and the Regiment moved to Dover as ordered. They arrived there early the next morning, embarked at 9 am, but did not sail until 11.30 am, reaching Calais at 1.15pm on 22 May, where they disembarked and awaited the arrival and unloading of their tanks from the *City of Christchurch,* still in Southampton docks when they had left Dover. 3 RTR had been scheduled to move to France in mid-1940 with 1st Armoured Division and although their precise destination had not been decided, stores and equipment had been loaded in readiness for a routine – not operational – move. This was a lengthy procedure that required the barrels of the tank main armament and machine guns to be filled with mineral jelly and the ammunition packed separately in boxes. As the situation in Calais deteriorated these routine move procedures were to cause difficulties in unloading the tanks and making them ready for battle. The personnel and equipment of 229 Anti-Tank Battery, Royal Artillery, sailed with 3 RTR on *The Maid of Orleans*, a cross-channel ferry requisitioned by the Admiralty as troop transport, but in the haste to move and the lack of space on board, four of the battery's twelve guns had to be left behind.

Having disembarked and harboured his men in the sand dunes to the north east of the port, Lieutenant Colonel Keller set off to locate the area HQ and clarify his mission. After some time he found Colonel Holland, who ordered him to unload his tanks and equipment as soon as possible and await orders from GHQ; later that evening he met Lieutenant General Brownrigg, who directed him to make contact with 2nd Guards Brigade in Boulogne the following morning, 23 May, telling him that speed was a necessity. The *City of Christchurch* arrived in Calais at 4 am; the dockyard had been severely damaged by shell fire, and despite Colonel Holland's best efforts it was becoming ever more crowded as troops from all regiments continued to arrive with their transport ignoring the transit camps and seeking passage home. Large numbers of refugees milled about aimlessly, adding to the congestion.

Once the *City of Christchurch* was berthed, the unloading of 3 RTR tanks and equipment began immediately but it was clear it would take some time. Only two derricks were operating and 7,000 gallons of fuel in cans had to be unloaded from the hold before the tanks, vehicles, equipment and ammunition could be reached; inevitably, getting them operational would be a lengthy business.

As they were unloaded, the tanks were filled with petrol and their guns cleared of grease before moving to concentration areas to net in radios; it was clear to Lieutenant Colonel Keller that they would not be ready to deploy as a regiment until well after midday on 23 May at the earliest. To compound matters, the roads south-west of Calais in the direction of Boulogne were clogged with French military transport and refugees; so reaching 2nd Guards Brigade as he had been ordered would not be easy.

In southern England, 2 KRRC on *SS Royal Daffodil*, with 1 RB on *SS Archangel* and two transport vessels carrying their vehicles and HQ 30 Bde staff and equipment, sailed on 22 May across the Solent to the open sea and were escorted to Dover by two destroyers. On board a meal was served, after which all ranks bedded down as best they could in the cramped conditions. Officers were given a briefing on the situation, but the information was already out of date; the optimistic picture painted of only a few German light-armoured detachments having broken through the French to the Calais area in which the Battalion would be landed to mop up, was far from the truth. Most people had a comparatively restful night despite the limited space and enjoyed a full cooked breakfast before they pulled into Dover at 7 am the following day, 23 May, to await further orders, wondering if they would they sail to France or disembark and return once again to Dorset.

General Brownrigg had left France shortly after briefing Lieutenant Colonel Keller, and on arrival in Dover, met Brigadier Nicholson. He briefed him on the situation and ordered him to join up with 3 RTR on arrival in Calais and move to Boulogne as soon as possible to relieve the Garrison there. Nicholson sailed to Calais with these orders but received contradictory direction over the next two days until the evening of 25 May, when he was ordered to hold at all costs.

At 11 am, 2 KRRC Commanding Officer, Lieutenant Colonel Miller, appeared and hurried on board having received the order to sail to Calais, although whether to hold the port or move to Boulogne to relieve the Garrison there was unclear. Escorted by destroyers and on a calm sea those on board were having a hasty breakfast of biscuit and cold corned beef when the air raid alarm sounded, followed very quickly by the explosion of a bomb close by and the rattle of anti-aircraft fire as a German bomber was engaged. Shortly after, the sound of depth charges detonating in response to a submarine alert was another unpleasant experience – an introduction to war for all ranks packed together below deck.

Following a battalion Orders Group (O Group), company commanders were able to issue maps and brief their officers; as it was understood, the situation was that German light-armoured units had broken through in northern France and were believed to be approaching Calais already; the battalion task, therefore, was to attack their lines of communication. 2 KRRC and 1 RB reached Calais some two hours after setting sail from Dover, disembarked in heavy rain, loaded their rifles, and at 2.30 moved through the town north-eastward to the sand dunes to dig-in and await the arrival of their vehicles. Wearing greatcoats and full kit, including heavy packs, it was a tiring march enlivened by the occasional sound of small-arms fire in the distance, confirming that German advance units were already closing in on Calais. Orders were changed to reflect the developing situation and companies set off on some lengthy marches to block roads leading into the city.

The ships carrying the two battalions' vehicles took a long time to come alongside for unloading which was then slowed by a lack of stevedores and frequently interrupted by the appearance of enemy planes. These planes were usually on reconnaissance missions, but as they sometimes dropped bombs the French stevedores took cover every time an aircraft appeared. Brigadier Nicholson issued his orders at 4 pm, deploying 2 KRRC to cover approaches from the port to the coast on the west and 1 RB from the port to the coast on the east. Unloading went on all night with cranes being operated by Riflemen in the absence of stevedores, and as their equipment was unloaded the Scout Platoons were deployed into harbour areas in the surrounding open country. Those not tasked to establish roadblocks on the main routes to the port were able to bed down for the night, a welcome respite after the previous few days. Forward of them on the roads into Calais, now comparatively quiet, 1 QVR remained manning roadblocks to turn away unarmed Allied troops and all civilians. In the town itself many French soldiers had now taken shelter in cellars among civilians and thrown away their weapons, resigned to being taken prisoner.

As Brigadier Nicholson was holding his 'O' Group an order was received from London that, 'overriding all other considerations', 350,000 rations landed in Calais were to be delivered to Dunkirk. This seemed to have been drafted with little or no awareness of the confusion and surprise of the German breakthrough but was acted upon nevertheless and 3 RTR was ordered to deliver them.

In Calais, Lieutenant Colonel Keller was under the impression that once his Regiment was unloaded and ready to move he was to join 20 Guards Brigade in Boulogne. He had then received instructions to secure two bridges over the Aa Canal, only for this to be superseded by an order to move the Regiment 'at once' to St Omer. He sent out a patrol to check the route but it failed to make contact with the enemy and returned; the order was repeated and a second patrol sent out to check the route ran into enemy armour and was forced to return. Although unloading of his vehicles and tanks was ongoing, Lieutenant Colonel Keller decided to deploy all his available tanks in an effort to reach St Omer as he had been ordered. They set off but lost several tanks in a sharp engagement nine miles down the road at Guines and fell back on Calais at 9.30 that evening in the face of increasing numbers of enemy tanks. It was at this point that he received the order from HQ 30 Brigade to deliver the rations for the BEF to Dunkirk and sent a squadron to confirm and clear the road. But contact with it was lost; it was learned later that they had run into strong opposition and only three tanks managed to reach Dunkirk, the remainder being destroyed and the crews captured.

Unaware of the situation, and suspecting a failure of communications, 3 RTR sent another squadron with a company from 1 RB but they were stopped by the flank guard that had been deployed by 1st Panzer Division advancing to cut off the BEF retreat to the Channel and the attempt to reach Dunkirk was abandoned. Reduced to nine cruisers and twelve light tanks, 3 RTR fell back on Calais and were deployed in the city by HQ 30 Bde to be used in support and counter-attack roles wherever needed until, without the necessary spares available, they became non-runners and had to be abandoned. But the fighting was not all one sided; to the west and south-west, two Panzer Divisions probing towards Calais ran into unexpected resistance from a hastily improvised defence in Orphanage Farm,

Coulogne, where the Searchlight Battery acting as infantry, held up the German advance for five hours before being forced to retire into Calais.

Whether the seriousness of the situation was brought home to the War Office by the failure of 3 RTR to reach Dunkirk is not recorded, but in the early hours of the following day, 24 May, the Chief of the Imperial General Staff (CIGS) spoke by telephone to Brigadier Nicholson. Orders were given that evacuation 'in principle' had been decided upon; all fighting personnel were to remain 'for the time being', but non-fighting troops and the wounded were to be evacuated. Shortly after dawn that day the unloading of the KRRC vehicles and equipment had been completed, but it is probable that these 'evacuation orders' were the reason that 1 RB saw their ship sail back to England carrying wounded and non-combatants before unloading was complete, leaving them without most of their vehicles and ammunition for the battle ahead.

It was not appreciated by the War Office or Brigadier Nicholson that Calais had been cut off and the situation was already hopeless. Early in the morning of 24 May those coastal defence guns in the forts around the harbour that were able to traverse sufficiently and fire inland, a need not envisaged in their design, engaged the German artillery on the high ground at Coquelles, five miles to the south-west. The French gunners fired rapidly, expending 683 rounds out of a stock of 895 by 10 am; once it was clear that the guns would soon be unable to bear as the enemy encircled and closed on the town, they were spiked and the bastions evacuated.

Fort Nieulay, a mile west of the city, was manned by forty French soldiers and a handful of French Marines armed with two heavy machine guns and a 25mm anti-tank gun, as well as fifty Riflemen from 1 QVR who had been manning improvised and exposed roadblocks nearby. Although subjected to heavy artillery and mortar fire, this small garrison held out until late afternoon delaying a full German advance on Calais for several valuable hours.

The French gunners who had evacuated the other forts made their way to the harbour, from where they were expecting to be taken to Cherbourg by the French navy. Their arrival coincided with the evacuation of British non-fighting troops and led to the initial belief by some French officers that Calais was being abandoned, but once this misunderstanding was corrected a number of French officers and some 800 soldiers, resolved to join the defence and played a valuable part in the defence of Bastion 11.

At about 9 pm of 24 May, Brigadier Nicholson was told by the War Office that the decision to evacuate had been confirmed – but not before 7 am the following morning, 25 May. In preparation for a withdrawal HQ 30 Brigade gave preliminary orders that the outer perimeter was to be held, but shortened if necessary, by setting up a double ring of defensive positions based on the fortified walls of the town as the outer ring, and the canals and basins of the harbour area as the inner ring. No explosive was available to demolish bridges so they would be left intact. As these orders were being enacted another message was received from London: 'In spite of policy of evacuation given you this morning, British forces in your area now under command General Fagalde who has ordered no, repeat no, evacuation. This means that you must comply for the sake of Allied solidarity.'

General Fagalde, as Commander 16th Corps, Fr 7th Army, was commanding the Dunkirk western perimeter defence that held firm, enabling the BEF to be evacuated from the beaches. He was captured on 18 June, just four days before the signing of the Armistice Agreement between France and Germany, and imprisoned in Königstein Castle near Dresden, Germany, until the end of the war.

The task given to Brigadier Nicholson was to hold on as long as possible and thereafter, as the harbour was by then of no importance to the BEF, 'To select best position to fight to the end'; the message ended '48th Division started marching to your assistance this morning'. This latter part of the message was an unfortunate misinterpretation of an order given to 48th Division to form a new defence line along the canal between St Omer and the coast thirty miles away that illustrates how unclear London was of the situation in northern France.

During these exchanges of signals between London and Calais, the unloading of 2 KRRC and 1 RB equipment and stores continued and, despite intermittent bombing and infrequent shelling, was completed shortly after dawn on 24 May, enabling the rifle companies to move to defensive positions around the city. 1 RB was deployed from the south of the port eastwards to the coast, while 2 KRRC was deployed on the western side covering the south west and south approaches. For 2 KRRC the areas that had to be covered were considerable; interlocking arcs of fire between companies and even at platoon level were impossible, so Scout Platoons were deployed to cover the gaps and link companies by patrolling forward.

Mike's platoon was sent to cover the area between 'B' Company in the centre and 'D' Company on their left (east); in his typical methodical and thorough way he visited both companies to check the accuracy of the positions he had marked in chinagraph on a large map board. Second Lieutenant Dick Scott, with three carriers from B Company, had been sent southwest to Coquelles at dawn to confirm if the enemy had occupied the village. Just after 7 am, they were fired on and the two leading carriers destroyed. Dick, although wounded in the leg, managed to jump out and made his way to Fort Nieulay by crawling along ditches to rejoin the fight, killing a German on the way with his pistol. 2 KRRC began to take casualties as the Germans probed forward and the battle developed; shelling became heavier and tank-led attacks triggered desperate fighting throughout the rest of the day. Naval gunfire support for the defenders was provided by the British destroyers *Vimiera*, *Verity* and *Wessex*, along with the Polish warship *Burza; at* 4 pm *in the afternoon* these vessels opened fire on an armoured column at Sangatte Hill, west of Calais, but were quickly attacked by a number of German airplanes. *Wessex* was sunk and *Burza* badly damaged before, having dropped all their bombs, the Stuka attack was broken off; one German airplane was shot down during the action. In the town fierce fighting continued; most of the Green Jackets' transport had been destroyed by shell fire and communications were down, thirst was a problem and ammunition already running low. The efforts of the defence had, however, caused the Germans to pause. The War Diary of 10 Panzer records: 'enemy resistance from scarcely perceptible positions was so strong that it was only possible to achieve quite slight local success'. Their evening situation report stated that one third of their equipment, vehicles and personnel, and half of their tanks, were casualties, and the troops were exhausted. As dusk was falling six Royal Navy Swordfish biplanes appeared and dropped several loads of bombs; although their target was out of their sight, for the Riflemen to see air support was reassuring.

Second Searchlight Battery commanded by Lieutenant Airey Neave had been incorporated into 'B' Company after withdrawing from Orphanage Farm and were fighting alongside the Riflemen in the Rue Edgar Quinet when Neave was wounded on the afternoon of 24 May. A Carrier commanded by Mike appeared, on his way to support 'D' Company. Seeing Neave was wounded, Mike directed him to a van flying a Red Cross before going on with his platoon to hold a very exposed position south-west of Calais and play an important part in preventing a German breakthrough. Neave was taken to the regimental aid-post and thence into the French military hospital where he underwent an operation; he later tried to make his way to the quay area in the hope of reaching a boat and returning to England but was unsuccessful and was taken prisoner.

In Calais, Brigadier Nicholson was concerned that the anti-tank weapons he had were proving ineffective. On hearing of this Churchill directed that naval 12-pounders should be sent over mounted on lorries. Vice Admiral Somerville, who had been on the retired list at the outbreak of war but volunteered for service and was appointed Director Anti-Aircraft Weapons and Devices, believed it was already too late to get the guns to Calais but decided to go over to the port and see for himself. Shortly before embarking he received a telephone message from the Prime Minister; circumstances had changed and he was directed to inform Brigadier Nicholson that Calais should be held 'to the last'; bearing this unpalatable message he crossed the Channel aboard the destroyer *Verity* with eighty Royal Marines and a quantity of ammunition, arriving at 1.30 in the morning of 25 May. On disembarking he located HQ 30 Bde in cellars under the Gare Maritime, 'lit by a few candles and filled with exhausted officers and men fast asleep except for the Staff Officers and telephonists actually on duty'. He woke the Brigadier who immediately asked if he had come to evacuate them. Somerville delivered the order that Calais was to be held 'to the last' to delay the German advance threatening to cut off the BEF from Dunkirk. Seemingly unperturbed, Nicholson said he had anticipated such orders and outlined his plan to withdraw to the Citadel and hold out there for as long as possible. Somerville returned to Dover on board another destroyer, *Wolfhound,* to report that he had spoken with Nicholson and the message had been delivered. A few days later, in a radio broadcast on 30 May Somerville described his visit and admiration for Brigadier Nicholson who had 'a quiet confidence and grim determination to hold out to the last man. No thought of surrender, no thought but to serve their country to the utmost of their endeavour and to the last man.' (Annex A)

At 11 am, an armoured car flying a white flag approached the south end of the Pont Georges Cinq, it was carrying the Mayor of Calais and an interpreter with a message for Brigadier Nicholson offering him the chance to surrender; they were taken to Brigade HQ, by then in the Citadel, to deliver their message. 'Surrender,' Nicholson is reported to have said. 'No, I shall not surrender. If the Germans want Calais they will have to fight for it.'

At about 1 pm, Ronnie Littledale (a 60th officer who had been commanding 'A' Company 2 KRRC until January 1940, when he was posted to 30 Brigade as the Transport Officer in the Brigade Logistic Headquarters that was now established in the Gare Maritime) arrived at 2 KRRC battalion headquarters. He had been instructed to collect petrol and deliver it to the tanks in the KRRC area but could not locate them and so handed over the fuel to HQ 2 KRRC before returning to the Gare Maritime. Just before he had set out, Logistic Headquarters had received orders to reinforce, 'immediately', a company of 1 RB outside the Gare Maritime, but despite going to both 1 RB and the Gare Maritime he could find no trace of them. Logistic HQ had in fact moved into the cellars underneath the station. Unable to find them he decided to head to Fort Risban at the harbour mouth where he was captured by a German patrol the next morning, almost naked, after swimming across a creek while trying to find friendly forces. He was to become a persistent escaper whose story is linked closely with that of Mike.

Around 4 am on 25 May, Scout platoons were sent forward; if no Germans were met the intention was to occupy delaying positions on the approach roads to the port area; Mike was sent out first. Crossing the Pont Jacquard and probing forward cautiously he saw German infantry, and at the same moment an anti-tank shell hit and disabled his carrier; as he bailed out his revolver lanyard snagged on the vehicle but he wrenched himself free, took over one of his section vehicles and made his way back to regimental headquarters for further orders. He was deployed to the southwest and was largely responsible for preventing any German breakthrough in that area.

There was fierce fighting throughout the day as German troops pushed forward against the bridges held by 2 KRRC that led to the citadel and port areas of the town. Platoons took over houses along the front line turning out the occupants and barricading the buildings. Rations, tea and cigarettes were brought around for the Riflemen and somehow the Officers' Mess staff managed to set up a long table covered in a white cloth under some trees and serve large helpings of omelette to any officer fortunate enough to be passing by who could spare a few minutes. Around midday a number of small German planes flew over dropping leaflets exhorting the defenders to cease their resistance.

> *La ville de Calais est sommée de rendre immediatement. La garnison de la ville quittera la ville sens armes, les mains levées, dans le delai d'une heure, sur la route de Coquelles, dans la direction la ville sens de Coquelles. A toute résistance continuée sera repondu par de nouveaux lancements de bombes et par un bombardement avec la plus lourde artillerie.*
>
> *Le General cdt le corps d'armee.*
>
> (The city of Calais is ordered to surrender immediately. The garrison will leave the city without weapons, hands raised, within an hour, using the road to Coquelles in the direction of Coquelles. Any continued resistance will be met by renewed bombing and shelling by the heaviest artillery. General Officer Commanding.)

It was regarded as a good laugh by the Riflemen and boosted their morale; the lull in fighting had given them an opportunity to improve their positions, replenish ammunition, rest, eat and clean both weapons and themselves. The bombardment started promptly at four in the afternoon and lasted for two hours, the artillery fire being supplemented by mortars and bombing. Tanks then advanced on the bridges, but despite heavy casualties and exhaustion the Riflemen held their positions and morale remained high; the limited amounts of food and ammunition available were distributed and where possible, the wounded were moved to the local hospital. Defences were improved in readiness for another day of battle.

At 1.30 am on the 26 May, Brigadier Nicholson arrived at Battalion HQ with a message from the Secretary of State for War:

> Defence of Calais to the utmost is of highest importance to our country as symbolising our continued cooperation with France. The eyes of the Empire are upon the defence

> of Calais, and HM Government are confident that you and your gallant regiments will perform an exploit worthy of the British name.

He gave instructions that, if the present positions could not be held, the Battalion was to withdraw to the Citadel and there make a final stand.

By 4.30 am of 26 May all companies were 'stood to' awaiting attack. It came soon after first light. German records show an artillery concentration of twenty-two 105mm and eighteen 150mm guns, with a battalion of six 210mm heavy howitzers, to fire 260lb HE shells onto the citadel. After a 70-minute artillery barrage, and with fire support from their armoured vehicles, the infantry would attack Fort Risban from the west and the canal bridges from the south to force an entry into the old town and harbour area. Motorcycle infantry and armoured cars of *Aufklärung Abteilung 90* (Reconnaissance Unit 90) would give fire support initially, followed around 7.30 am by two hours of Stukas wailing unnervingly in their dive-bombing attack, the noise coming from a small propeller attached to the landing legs of the aircraft when it reached a certain speed in a dive. They came in waves of thirty to fifty aircraft and set many buildings on fire as the German infantry looked on.

> With deafening crashes bomb after bomb does destructive work. Red flames flicker in various place, thick smoke and sand clouds rise skywards and large chunks of masonry spin through the air ... the preparation for the attack is rounded off by artillery ... the instant the last shell lands our men charge forward into the attack ... initial successes are reported ... but the enemy has come back to life ... individual groups of shock troops penetrate the citadel but are pushed back by a British counterattack almost to their starting point.[1]

After a pause to regroup, German troops renewed their attacks and gradually began to overwhelm the defenders as casualties increased and ammunition ran low. By midday many of the forward positions had had to be abandoned and the defence drawn back to the area of the harbour, main square and cathedral, hampered by numbers of French soldiers milling around waiting to surrender. Barricades of debris were improvised and manned, but they proved no obstacle to the German tanks that were working their way forward and fragmenting the defence. The Regimental Aid Post (RAP) was withdrawn to the tunnel under the citadel already crammed with men from various units sheltering from the fighting and with many wounded in the side chambers where, in scenes reminiscent of an earlier age, a shortage of equipment forced the doctors to use a hacksaw blade they found and sterilised, to carry out amputations.

Above the tunnel and in the port area small parties of determined young officers and riflemen became isolated, but fought on if necessary fixing 'swords', as bayonets are known by Green Jackets, to mount counter attacks and prevent their positions being overrun. Resistance only ended when ammunition ran out and there were undoubtedly acts of heroism that, never witnessed, went unrewarded.

Pulling back to the citadel, Phil Pardoe met Lieutenant Colonel Miller, Alick Williams the Adjutant, and Mike – the latter filthy dirty with four days' growth of beard – and was directed to assemble 'C' Company to form a rearguard in the street with his platoon. Shortly after, he saw movement on the cliffs to his right and realised the Germans had broken through; at the same moment, Lieutenant Colonel Miller reappeared to say the Battalion was surrounded and further organised resistance was impossible; the Battalion was to divide into small parties to escape, 'every man for himself'. The Riflemen did so, but all save a handful were soon rounded up and forced to surrender. The few remaining tanks of 3 RTR withdrew eastwards through the sand dunes north of the Bassin des Chasses until they broke down or ran out of fuel and were destroyed by their crews, who then joined the Riflemen attempting to avoid capture. Lieutenant Colonel Keller and a small group managed to make their way along the shoreline to Gravelines where they made contact with French troops; they were then able to reach Dunkirk and were evacuated to England.

In the confusion and inevitable separation of the battle, Gris lost contact with his platoon positions. Unaware of the order to disperse and make their way out of Calais as best they could, he set off to locate his riflemen and rally the defence. He describes in his account of the battle how, while standing near the canal and looking about, he came under fire, was hit in several places and badly wounded. After lying unconscious for some hours, by which time the fighting had ended, he regained his senses and managed to tie his field dressing around his head wound before dragging himself to a hut where he passed out, to be woken sometime later by a German soldier searching the area. '*Verwundet?*' he was asked; on replying '*Ja, verwundet*', the German examined Gris' wounds and used his own field dressing to bind round his head before leaving with the assurance that *'hilfe kommt'*. Gris was collected a short time later by two Germans and managed with their help to make his way to one of their medical posts. It was the evening of 26 May. His story as a POW after recovering is closely linked with that of Mike, with whom he was a close friend.

Apart from the Fleet Air Arm bombing raid at dusk on 24 May, the Luftwaffe appeared to dominate the sky over Calais, causing some bitter comments from the Riflemen fighting in the city to whom the air support they received was not readily apparent. Calais was within the range of RAF aircraft based in Britain but they had insufficient fuel to loiter over the French coast if they were to return to their airfields. Many engagements took place inland out of sight of those fighting below; on 22 May, Hurricanes and Spitfires shot down two Junkers 88 bombers and claimed a further five Messerschmitt 109s for the loss of three Spitfires. From 21–22 May, Luftwaffe losses over the Channel ports were 15, against RAF losses of six fighters and 13 bombers. On 26 May, 613 Squadron, in the process of converting from Hector bi-planes to Lysanders, flew in support of the forces in Calais and dive-bombed German positions around the port. Then, at first light on 27 May, in response to a request from the War Office received the previous evening, and unaware that even before the request was made the Citadel had fallen, 12 Lysanders dropped supplies of water in Calais; a few hours later, at 10 am, a further 17 Lysanders dropped supplies of ammunition in the Citadel while nine Fleet Air Arm Swordfish bombed enemy artillery near the town. Three Lysanders were lost on the two missions and one of the Hectors, that had accompanied the Swordfish, crashed at Dover.

On 26 and 27 May a number of small boats went into the harbour and brought away wounded. A group of 46 men hidden under the pier and undiscovered by the Germans managed to signal out to sea with an aldis lamp; remarkably, the signal was picked up and HM Yacht *Gulzar* which returned after dark in a last search for survivors. She was spotted, came under fire and was in the process of putting back to sea when shouts from under the pier brought her round. The yacht could not stop and the survivors were told to 'jump for it' as the *Gulzar* went by. Forty-seven men did so and reached Dover safely.

As the survivors were gathered up by the Germans in Calais, despite many gallant attempts, only a handful of Officers and Riflemen managed to escape and make their way back across the Channel. Second Lieutenant Lucas, QVR, rowed to England alone in a dinghy, and Captain Alick Williams, Adjutant 2 KRRC, slipped away from the column of prisoners being marched off after the battle and after many adventures reached England. These two escapes illustrate the truth of what is taught in the British Army that no matter how hard the fight may have been, it is best to attempt escape as soon as possible after capture when, despite battle fatigue, you are likely to be in better physical condition and closer to friendly forces than you will be again, even a short time later. In Calais this was certainly the case, those captured were rounded up tired, thirsty and bemused; as Phil Pardoe recalled, 'everyone moved as in a dream and the immediate future was impossible to contemplate.'[2]

The losses in 2 KRRC were nine officers killed and seven wounded, 120 other ranks killed and around 200 wounded. Among those rounded up and marched away was Mike, exhausted and filthy dirty from the battle in which he had played an important part – recognised by the award of a Mention in Dispatches (MID) 'for gallant and distinguished service in the defence of Calais'. His attempts to escape and return to active service would soon begin.

CHAPTER 3

FIRST DAYS AS A PRISONER OF WAR

THE MARCH FROM CALAIS

On British Army 'Conduct after Capture' courses it is emphasised that it becomes increasingly difficult to escape the longer you remain a prisoner; your best chance of getting away, even if you are fatigued thirsty and hungry, is as soon after capture as possible so seize the first, or any, chance that comes along. In Calais on 25 May, as the Germans overcame the last resistance and took possession of the city, most of the defenders whether Riflemen, Gunners, Marines or French, were exhausted, filthy, hungry and thirsty; a sudden, apathy and an overwhelming desire for sleep pushed aside any thoughts of escape. For the British in particular the sight of the evening sun on the white cliffs of Dover, from where they had left in high spirits only days before, was tantalising – but exhaustion was their overwhelming sensation. In four days of fighting, indeed since being ordered to move to Southampton on 21 May then sailing to Dover and across to Calais on the 23rd, there had been little rest, and even less sleep, for the Riflemen.

The initial reaction to capture was utter weariness, despair and indifference tempered by a slowly dawning realisation of what defeat implied for them. Bodies, some dead for a number of days and now swollen in the heat and beginning to decompose, lay around with the sickly sweet smell of putrefaction hanging in the air, an odour once encountered never forgotten. Around the area of the Citadel and harbour basin, buildings were shattered and smouldering, the streets strewn with glass, wrecked vehicles and abandoned equipment. A number of the defeated Riflemen were set to work in groups collecting and burying the dead, a ghastly job, the corpses rigid with expressions fixed at the moment of death, some burnt beyond recognition, some already decomposing and having to be carried on shovels to improvised graves. Trying to identify the bodies was an unpleasant business since in many cases the pressed fibre identity (ID) discs that each man carried, and should have been wearing around the neck, had instead been put in their pockets and could only be found by searching the corpses. The purpose of these discs was to enable identification of the body for formal interment at a later date; regulations required one ID disk to be attached to the corpse the other to be sent up the administrative chain of command so that accurate casualty lists could be compiled but in the prevailing circumstances, with neither an operational nor administrative chain of command, such niceties were impossible. Where they could, the burial parties scratched the names of those they recognised on rough homemade crosses and attached the ID discs to the bodies as they were buried in the shallow graves that were all they were able to dig. To their surprise and gratitude, on completion of their task, the burial parties were given soap and towels and were able to wash in water flowing from shattered pipes into the streets. The behaviour of the German front-line troops towards their prisoners was exemplary, showing a total lack of discrimination between wounded friend or foe, as Gris had already experienced; they were correct and embarrassingly friendly, engaging the Riflemen in conversation and giving them food and cigarettes. Phil Pardoe, who had managed to get some wine from them to quench the thirst of the burial party he had been working with, was approached by one who pointed to his shoulder badge and said ‘KRR – King’s Royal Rifle Corps – *sehr gute* Regiment’, seemingly harking back to the origins of the Regiment and the German and Swiss settlers in north America, from among whom it was first raised. The attitude of these front-line troops served to dissuade thoughts of any immediate attempt to escape and would prove to be markedly different to those farther back from the front. Shouting, bullying and general unpleasantness seemed natural to the German second-line troops; regrettably it would soon become the normal behaviour expected by the prisoners from their captors, who seemed convinced that if they shouted loudly enough they would be understood.

As the defeated Riflemen were formed up to be marched out of the town they were joined by hundreds of French soldiers emerging from the cellars where they had been sheltering waiting for the fighting to end. To the Riflemen, most of them looked fresh and in good spirits, many were clean shaven carrying large suitcases or wearing bulging rucksacks festooned with pots, pans and other assorted impedimenta that they clearly thought might prove useful in the uncertain days ahead. In stark contrast, the majority of the captured Riflemen had been searched thoroughly and relieved of whatever meagre possessions they had been carrying in their stripped-down fighting order of ammunition pouches and basic webbing; the greatcoats and large packs, containing washing and shaving gear, spare clothing and personal effects with which they had set out from Essex were cumbersome, and believing they would be a hindrance in the anticipated street fighting, had been left in platoon or company locations for retrieval later. Despite being searched some managed to secrete any small treasures they still possessed about their person, in socks, boots and even in their mouths. Inevitably resentment of the French built up, fomented by the Germans who seemed to be following a policy of divide and rule – although whether deliberately or not was unclear. To them, the French were already a beaten nation and there was little point in treating them too harshly.

That night Mike and others from 2 KRRC were held in the Eglise Notre Dame in central Calais which had survived the battle largely undamaged and was serving as a temporary prison; it was crowded with French troops, many of whom grouped together to pool what bread, cheese and wine they had managed to carry with them into captivity, but steadfastly refused to share with the British and stayed in their groups for protection. There were water taps inside the church, but it was a struggle to get a drink with so many men desperate to slake their thirst and fill whatever, if any, receptacle they possessed. An unpleasant consequence of so many men being crowded together was the lack of enough latrines to answer the inevitable calls of nature. The French appeared to have lost any sense of what in the British Manual of Military Law is referred to as 'good order and military discipline', basic hygiene was ignored and they relieved themselves wherever they were lying. Consequently, urine and excrement littered the floor haphazardly making it difficult to find enough unfouled space to lie down. Despite their hunger and thirst, battle fatigue, exhaustion and the need to sleep after four days of fighting overwhelmed everything else; the Riflemen found what space they could to lie down and were quickly asleep.

Waking the next morning, 26 May, individuals began to explore their 'prison' and it was with delight, while doing so, that Phil Pardoe bumped into Mike; they exchanged what news they had of their brother officers in the Regiment who also had survived the fighting, and of those they knew had been killed. Around 11 am, the Germans began to rouse their prisoners and marshal them for the day's march; there had been no food or water issued so the POWs scrounged around for both and anything else that might prove of value in the uncertain days ahead. Mike and Phil Pardoe joined up with a number of other 2 KRRC officers, among them Derek Trotter and Godfrey Cromwell – the latter blind in one eye and limping from a wounded leg, but keeping going and ever cheerful. It was soon apparent that the troops who had captured them, or to whom they had surrendered in Calais, had been replaced and the front line comradeship of shared battle experience was gone; the troops now guarding them seemed full of hate and contempt. The Riflemen set off in a column predominately of French troops, and about a mile long, guarded by Germans riding bicycles with a truck mounting a machine gun bringing up the rear, serving the dual purpose of deterring any individual thinking of making a break for freedom and of picking up stragglers genuinely incapable of walking further. Despite the guards, whenever there was an opportunity, bold and enterprising individuals ducked away from the column to forage in the abandoned houses and gardens they were passing for scraps of food, or scavenge in the fields for potatoes, swedes or anything edible, until a burst of machine-gun fire over their heads brought them back into line or irate guards descended on them and with a sharp thump from a rifle butt encouraged them back to the rest. It was noticeable to the Riflemen that when passing through villages the guards would turn a blind eye to French prisoners breaking ranks to buy whatever they could in the local shops but would tighten their control of the British to prevent any attempt to do the same.

Mixed columns of French, Belgian, Dutch and British prisoners had started their march into captivity shortly after dawn from locations across the northern part of France. The offensive southwards against the French Weygand Line, and from there onwards to Paris, was the point of main effort for the German forces; their movement was rapid and they took a huge number of prisoners creating the problem of how to guard, feed and move them to the rear, certainly no front-line troops could be spared as all vehicles and men were needed for the continuing advance south. To resolve their dilemma the German High Command took the decision that the POWs should be marched daily on circuitous routes from town to town, well behind the front line, keeping them in a state of semi-exhaustion without any energy to devote to escape, and guarded by the *Feldgendarmerie* (Military Police). The problem of feeding them was left to the Red Cross, who were instructed by the German authorities 'to provide food wherever possible'. While not strictly in accordance with the Geneva Convention on the treatment of POWs that stipulated they must be given adequate food, clothing, housing, and medical attention, it was a pragmatic decision in their eyes.

When responsibility for guarding the prisoners was handed over from the Wehrmacht, the affinity the Riflemen had shared with their captors was effectively ended. Now if a prisoner wandered out of line or fell behind he was helped along and encouraged to catch up with the occasional blow from a rifle butt, causing the whole column to begin stumbling forward faster to the amusement of their captors. Kept semi-exhausted and underfed, marching twelve to twenty miles a day from shortly after dawn to late afternoon, thoughts of escape were quickly pushed aside by the effort needed to keep going. The routine for the POWs was to rouse at four or five in the morning, from wherever they had managed to find a spot to lie down at the end of the previous day's march, with twenty minutes allowed to line up ready to move; a cup of acorn coffee was occasionally provided but nothing to eat. They stepped off for the day's march at a pace that was dictated by fatigue and misery and usually less than two miles per hour, halting every one or two hours for up to thirty minutes – a false kindness, if kindness it was intended to be, as legs tended to seize up after ten minutes of rest and getting going again was a painful process. By 8 or 9 am it would be getting hot; water was usually available at halts, but not always, and any of the locals who failed to get permission before offering water to the marching prisoners frequently had it dashed from their hands by the guards, while those who tried to hand out food ran the risk of a clubbing with rifle butts. In one village an elderly grey-haired lady, holding out her apron filled with pieces of bread for the passing prisoners, was knocked to the ground by a guard and kicked, to the fury of the impotent British. The POWs walked in silence for the most part, wrapped in their own thoughts; many suffered blisters but received no help and were jeered at by the guards if they fell out. It became a matter of pride for the British officers and men to plod on no matter how footsore, rather than fall out and suffer the same humiliation. Usually around three or four in the afternoon the day's march would end at a town where, if they were in luck, there was a roof over their heads for the night.

Despite the conditions the soldiers kept their sense of humour and ability to laugh at their predicament. In his memoir Ted Taylor, a Rifleman in 1 RB, recounts meeting two soldiers from the Royal Sussex who had been captured in the retreat to Dunkirk. They asked him how long he had been in France:

> 'Don't know, what's the date today?'
> '29th of May I think,' came the reply.
> 'I think we got here on the 24th'.
> 'Oh, just weekend trippers then, hardly worth coming was it!'

It was a joke that stuck with Taylor, and in later years provided him with a title for his memoir: The *Weekend Trippers*.

In the company of the little group of 2 KRRC officers that had formed, Mike and other British prisoners were at the rear of an ever-growing column of predominantly French captives that halted for the night of 26 May at a church in Guines after their first day's march of about 12 miles. Being at the front the French were first into the building that filled up rapidly, leaving room for only a few of the British, among them the group of 2 KRRC officers, the remainder having to bed down in the graveyard. Once locked in for the night they had an opportunity to consider the situation and their prospects of escape, although their most immediate thoughts were of food and how to satisfy the gnawing hunger they all felt. They were given some biscuits by the Germans and Derek Trotter shared out the meagre amount of chocolate he had left. Neither did much to satisfy their hunger – but fatigue, not hunger, was the predominant feature of their existence; it affected their judgement and lured them to the simpler, and in their circumstances easier, 'wait and see' course of action, for surely the French would hold a defensive line on the Somme and the Allies would counterattack. Better therefore, they concluded, to delay any attempt to escape until a more favourable time, especially given the question of what action the Germans might take if one was recaptured.

After a fitful night the POWs were roused the next morning, 27 May, by shouts of '*Los! Los! Aus, schneller! Raus, Raus*', and prodded into line by rifle butts for their second day's march. By now they were so many that the Germans separated them into smaller and more easily guarded columns on differing routes; the group of 2 KRRC officers were in a column that took them to Maquise after another long trek of 12 miles. There was no food or water provided as they marched, so many prisoners scooped up and drank what they could from ditches alongside the roads but often the brackish and dirty liquid would cause diarrhoea within a day or so, forcing them to squat at the roadside and endure the humiliation of their predicament and the mocking of the guards. Sometimes they were not allowed to stop to relieve themselves, so any who could no longer control their bowels had no alternative other than to foul themselves as they walked. Occasionally they were lucky enough to stumble across discarded or accidentally dropped items of food; these were treasure! On one occasion a small tin of OXO cubes provided a pint of thin but tasty broth; although when divided between a dozen or more the amount each person received was little more than a mouthful, it was welcome and nourishing. Old potatoes, bacon rind and anything else discovered on rubbish heaps was put to good use and stewed along with nutritious nettles and dandelion leaves. There were occasional lucky breaks for some; finds of half-eaten tins of food and discarded stale bread were quickly consumed and no opportunity to pilfer from those guarding them was missed. After a hot day and a slow, dispiriting march to Maquise, they again spent the night in a church where Phil found a comfortable if irreverent spot stretched out on the altar with his fellow officers lying on the steps below him.

They were roused at 4 am in the morning and set off on their third day of marching, a 25-mile hike that was to last until late afternoon that day, 28 May, when they entered a greyhound stadium in Le Wast along with several thousand others from many different units. It began to rain. Pushing their way through the crowds to the grandstand where they hoped to get some shelter, they met up with a dozen of their fellow officers from 2 KRRC, many of whom they had believed dead, but their delight at this unexpected reunion was diminished by learning of those who had been killed or whose fate was not known. Their exchange of news was cut short by realisation that a hot meal was being provided by the Red Cross; joining the queues they each received a small portion of stew; they suspected from the aroma that the meat was horse, but no less welcome for that and in their circumstances a great luxury. It continued to rain and they realised as they were moved out of the stadium, and into a much longer column than the one in which they had arrived, that contrary to their hopes the day's march was not over. Their trek resumed and 12 miles later, still in the rain, they arrived at Hucqueliers where they spent the night, the officers once again shut in a church. The local priest arrived bringing very welcome contributions of food from the whole village for the POWs; the 2 KRRC officers were doubly blessed when a little later a French officer befriended them and brought them a little hot soup and some pâté sandwiches. While most of the rest of the column spent a miserable and wet night as best they could in the fields, a small group of enterprising QVR Riflemen found a large carpet and some canvas among the litter that they used to make a waterproof and snug bed; despite the downpour they slept soundly through the night.

Their good fortune continued the next morning, 29 May, when the villagers came out to give them water, red wine and anything they could spare, as the column set out at 6 am on the day's march. Those who had endured the night in the open were soaked through but soon their clothes were steaming as the sun rose and it turned very hot, making this fourth day of marching more tiring than ever and the POWs increasingly thirsty. In most of the villages they passed through the women produced buckets of water from which both the French and British were able to fill their water bottles or whatever receptacle they had acquired; occasionally a little food was given out or could be bought by whoever was passing with no apparent preference given to either French or British. It was shortly after setting out from Hucqueliers that Alick Williams, the Adjutant of 2 KRRC, and Tony Rolt, a platoon commander from 1 RB, managed to slip away from the column unseen. Tony Rolt was quickly picked up but Alick Williams evaded capture and managed to reach the coast, meeting on the way two officers from HQ 30 Bde, the BM, Captain Talbot and the Brigade Signals Officer, Lieutenant Millett. After nearly three weeks on the run these three linked up with two French Officers and four soldiers who had acquired a small cabin cruiser and were intent on escaping to England. The engine proved temperamental but after several days and some false starts they finally got it going and were able to set out for Dover on 16 June, nursing it along only for it to fail *the following evening when about eight miles out from Folkestone.* Despite their best efforts it would not restart so they hoisted a *makeshift distress signal on an oar; half an hour later a Royal Navy destroyer made a welcome appearance to take them on board and land them in England.*

At around 4.30 on 29 May the column stopped for the night in Hesdin where those who still had some money clubbed together and were able to buy food from the locals. Mike and Phil kept together and shared whatever they could get; there was never a great deal on offer but any milk, butter or cheese was welcome. The officers spent the night in comparative comfort in the stables of an abandoned Chateau enjoying having straw for bedding and access to running water.

Setting out the next day – 30 May and the fifth of their march – the general direction changed and the column began to head east. Walking through the Forêt d'Hesdin a number of individuals took the opportunity to slip away into the trees but the majority, Mike and his fellow officers from 2 KRRC included, walked on wrapped in their own misery and thoughts, ignoring the slim opportunity for escape that the forest offered. The POWs reached Doullens where they came within earshot of artillery fire in the direction of Abbeville, which they guessed was where the front line now lay, but they were too fatigued and lethargic to try to slip away. While the remainder of the column were herded into a civil prison, the officers were shut in what they believed had been a girls' school; they were right in a sense as the sign outside read '*L'école pour la preservation des jeunes filles*' – in other words, a reform school for prostitutes! In the civil prison queues quickly formed around the outside water taps, while numerous French soldiers crowded against the railings trying to converse with individuals in the mass of women that had appeared outside, desperately calling for news of husbands, brothers or sons. Food in the form of watery soup and biscuits was provided for the British once the French had been fed and before all the prisoners were herded towards the buildings for the night. The difficulty of finding a clear place to lie down and sleep once inside, was compounded by the number of prisoners suffering from dysentery and forced to squat wherever they could when the need was pressing. Some of the cell floors were covered with several inches of excreta and the stench in the heat was vile.

For the officers conditions were easier and the next day a number including Phil, were detailed to join a group being sent to a nearby farm to fill water bottles. There they found an old man who was willing to sell them some milk and who, on being asked if he had any food to sell, offered a live cockerel which they purchased immediately. The officers set about trying to wring its neck, but their amateur efforts were interrupted by a horrified Frenchman who insisted that unless bled out, the bird would be inedible and then, seeing their mystified looks, did the job for them. The bird was then plucked and drawn ready for the pot, but they were roused and moved on again before they could cook it so their prize was thrust into a sack to be stewed and eaten later. Unexpectedly, they were moved by lorry; their destination, and where they spent the night of 31 May, their sixth day of marching, is not recorded, but given the description of the following day's trek and distances it is likely to have been in the area of Bapaume, from where they walked on to Cambrai on 1 June, their seventh day of marching. This was a long march in the hottest weather they had endured so far, at the end of which they suffered the humiliation of being paraded around the town, apparently 'on show'. Phil Pardoe, many years later, vividly recalled an old woman there who started throwing sweets into the column of prisoners: 'she was immediately surrounded by a hungry swarm of men all trying, like sharks, to snatch some food. The good lady was so badly crushed and frightened that she dropped the bag, burst into tears and was only extricated from the midst of this sordid rabble with difficulty.'

At Cambrai there was a camp with a semblance of organisation and the small group of officers were able to secure bunks and water. The chicken they had carried for a couple of days was finally roasted and shared out; although there was only sufficient for each of them to have a small piece, the taste to hungry men was exquisite and when they looked back on it 'the most wonderful moment of the whole march'.[1] They were left alone for the rest of the day providing a welcome chance to rest and with the availability of water to wash themselves as well as give their socks and clothes a perfunctory rinse. The following day, 2 June, the march resumed and the prisoners found themselves crossing the battlefields of the 1914–1918 war with their immaculately kept cemeteries and rows of crosses. The general direction the columns took was steadily northeast towards the Belgian frontier, and each march continued to be around 20 to 25 kilometres a day; it has not been possible to confirm exact dates and destinations day-by-day, but it is clear that circumstances did not improve. On most days when they arrived in a location that had already served as an overnight stopping-off point for other columns conditions were appalling; ditches had been used as latrines where possible, but for the most part prisoners had had to squat to relieve themselves wherever they could and the consequent swarms of flies and stench in the heat were nauseating. However, the few opportunities to wash themselves – let alone their clothes – in the days since they had landed in Calais meant that thanks to their own body odour the prisoners were by now largely immune to the pungent smell.[2]

Conditions did not improve as they marched on and it seemed that the further they moved from the front the less well (with some exceptions) they were treated by their guards. The meagre rations they received were still supplemented by anything they could pick up as they marched; if they passed a field of vegetables, prisoners darted off to grab what they could – notwithstanding the risk of being shot – hedges were stripped of leaves and verges of dandelions to assuage their hunger. Lieutenant Colonel Miller, with Mike as interpreter, spoke with German officers about improving conditions but his requests and complaints were ignored. In an apparent attempt to worsen relations between the French and British prisoners, whenever a meal was provided the Germans would call forward the French first often leaving very little, sometimes nothing, for the British.

The march continued and without maps the prisoners had little idea of where they might be; the effort needed to keep going became all-consuming and any idea of escape slipped further away as they slowly became more and more focused on their stomachs. Further discouragement came when word went around from their captors that anyone trying to leave the column, or found in civilian clothes, was likely to be shot as a spy. They crossed the Belgium frontier and marched on for several days through the hilly Ardennes, where generous villagers gave them whatever food they could spare. All were footsore and by now several were suffering from blisters, in particular Ronnie Littledale, who had been kitted out with whatever was available after his capture on 25 May near naked, after swimming across a creek attempting to reach 30 Brigade Logistics HQ, and Mike who was plagued by rheumatism. In all, their march into captivity lasted about two weeks and covered 180 miles before reaching Bastogne railway station where they boarded cattle trucks that were marked '*Hommes 40 Chevaux 8*' – (40 men or 8 Horses).

Despite this regulation around sixty prisoners were crammed into each car making it impossible to sit down unless they organised themselves so that half were standing and half sitting in turn. Night brought some relief from the heat but there was little ventilation and the atmosphere in the wagon quickly became fetid as those suffering from diarrhoea, unable to control their bowels, were forced to soil themselves. A few individuals had retained their tin helmets that were used and emptied out of the small grilles high up on sides of the wagons, but for most the sudden need to relieve themselves was uncontrollable. Occasionally during the night the trains were shunted into sidings to allow military rail traffic to pass, but it was not until the early hours of the following day that their journey ended in Trier, Germany, where they dismounted and made a short, steep climb to the camp overlooking the town.

The camp held many thousands of French and British troops housed in insect-infested buildings; the officers, however, were taken to a large and clean building where they spent several days mostly lying on their beds recovering from the long march. They were given the opportunity to write to their families but they could say nothing about their experiences so their letters were largely a list of those they knew had been casualties, with a catalogue of what they hoped could be sent to them, mainly food. They were assembled daily and marched to the main camp for a midday bowl of soup; being officers they were not required to queue with the ORs but nevertheless were able to contact some of the Riflemen and get news of casualties. There was also a canteen where those still with money were able to buy a few items including lavatory paper, a very welcome purchase. Although they knew little of the area the news spread that they were going to

Laufen in Bavaria and it was welcomed; the Alps was a picturesque destination to which they looked forward. Their journey started a week later when they left Trier by train for a short and comparatively comfortable journey to Mainz, where they passed four quiet days, largely on their beds except for meals.

The wounded from the Calais battle who could move, among them Gris, were assembled after the capture of the port and made their way slowly and painfully to a church now serving as a field hospital, where they were divided into lightly, average and severely wounded. The British walking wounded were moved to a small hospital run by British doctors and padres with the help of some French nurses, where Gris was put to bed. Rumours were rife and, appreciating the worry that news of the fall of Calais would cause his family, he completed a special POW postcard that stated 'I am a prisoner of war. I am well/unwell' and sent it off. Six weeks later it was delivered, ending the agonising wait for news his mother in particular was enduring. For the families of those being marched across France the wait for news was equally hard with only Alick Williams able to provide what limited information he had after reaching England.

In Calais the lightly wounded were moved out of hospital and walked slowly under escort through the ruined town to a large square where, after a long wait, they were allocated space in a ruined flat in the citadel that had once been a married quarter. As experienced by other prisoners, the British were made to wait at meal-times until all the French had been served. After a few days the wounded were driven to a transit camp at Cotillon where Gris saw a French military doctor who pronounced his arm to be badly infected. To remove the poison, he twisted the arm as if wringing out a cloth, causing excruciating pain as poison squirted out of the entry and exit wounds; he examined and dressed Gris' head wound, telling him that he was lucky as the bullet had missed his eye on entry and spinal column on exit by a fraction. After a couple of nights, he was moved on again by lorry and then train, arriving on 9 June at Mainz, where the camp housed French and British officers. Looking around he was amazed to see two brother officers from 2 KRRC, Jack Poole and Wally Finlayson, staring at him – a figure in a dirty bloodstained battledress bulging with bandages, with his head covered in a turban-like swathe of dressings. Gris recalled what followed:

> 'Good Lord Jack, that's Gris'.
>
> 'No old boy, it can't be, and you shouldn't say things like that. We both know he was killed. It looks a bit like him that's all.'
>
> At last I found my voice.
>
> 'Jack, Wally. It's me, it's Gris,' and they rushed over to where I stood.

In the company of the other 2 KRRC Officers in Mainz their short stay proved to be a time of reunion and news-gathering, a mixture of joy at the survival and sorrow at the death, of brother officers and fellow Riflemen.

Their onward move was again by cattle truck, but slightly less crowded than previously with around forty in each wagon allowing them some space to move around but still necessitating taking turns to lie down and sleep; for the wounded it was unpleasant and for Gris a painful experience whether lying down or taking his turn to stand. They were given a little bread, sausage and margarine for the two-day journey, but thirst rather than hunger was their main concern; there were no sanitary arrangements so tin helmets were again put to use; playing cards improvised from biscuit cartons helped to pass the time until their arrival at the town of Laufen, Bavaria.

They emerged from the cattle trucks on 15 June with their few belongings and saw their destination: a square-shaped, forbidding building that overlooked the town from across a river. It was a short march over a bridge and then uphill to reach it, in all about two miles; although a relief to be in the fresh air, their poor physical state, and the cramped conditions of the previous two days and nights in the cattle wagons, made it a struggle. The building to which they were being marched was the castle built as a fortified residence for the Archbishop of Salzburg in the fifteenth century and now serving as an Officers prisoner of war camp designated Oflag VII-C.

CHAPTER 4

OFLAG VII – C

> 'Accommodation was disgracefully overcrowded and the food most inadequate until parcels arrived. The Commandant refused to consider the Geneva Convention or to supply a copy of it to the SBO.'
>
> Major Ronnie Littledale KRRC,
> report to MI9 following his 'home run' 1942

Any cheerful illusions the officers were harbouring about Laufen as a prison camp were quickly dispelled. As they struggled into the courtyard of the forbidding-looking buildings they were immediately searched and any fountain pens, knives and money they still possessed were taken. They were left in the hot sun for the rest of the morning until issued with a bowl, mug and simple eating implements of knife, fork and spoon, and given a drink of coffee with milk and saccharine, 'the best drink we had had since capture', thought Major Michael Duncan, before being herded back for the night into what appeared to have been a coach house at one time and given straw to lie on with a blanket for bedding.

The building, from which they were only allowed out under escort to use the latrines, was oppressively dark with just two small skylights; some British orderlies already in the newly established camp were permitted to bring them hot washing water but nothing else and were under strict orders not to take or deliver any messages.

After 36 hours in the coach house an English orderly was brought in to cut the officers' hair and then shave their heads under the supervision of the German camp authorities. Ostensibly this was to ensure that no prisoner had head lice, a reasonable explanation that would have been more convincing if their several weeks' growth of beard had been removed as well; most believed it to be an attempt by the camp authorities to humiliate them and break their morale, thereby making them less likely to attempt escape. Although they were left looking ludicrous, they were able to laugh at their appearance that was, after all, they decided, not so much different from the close cropped look of many of their guards. Oberst Frey, the camp Commandant, was a tall, pompous Prussian of about 70 who sported a monocle and clearly hated the British, using every excuse to reject any suggestions made by Brigadier Nicholson, as the Senior British Officer (SBO), to improve their conditions; Frey was assisted by six officers and two NCOs, who were separate from the camp guard force and conducted the day-to-day close supervision of the POWs. Any complaint made to them that their treatment of the prisoners was not in accordance with the Geneva Convention[1] was met with the terse response that it was the Weimar Government who had signed the Convention, not the Nazis.

Having had their heads shaved, the newly arrived officers, as the day before, spent the rest of the morning in the courtyard under a hot sun and were searched once more for anything that might have been missed previously. They were then issued with identity discs and intensively questioned before being given a very welcome meal of sauerkraut, a piece of sausage and two boiled potatoes. After eating they stripped off completely to be 'deloused', for most of them the first time they had been able to take their clothes off since setting out from Bury St Edmunds over a month earlier and were given a medical examination while their clothes were being baked to clear them of lice and eggs. Once their uniforms were returned and they had dressed, they were herded through into the main camp, with about 200 men pushed into each room for the night.

The rooms were 40ft by 20ft with beds in tiers of three, the bottom one 6in off the floor, the top one some 6ft higher, claustrophobically close to the ceiling, and only accessible by clambering up while being careful not to tread on the occupants of the lower levels. Bedding consisted of a palliasse and straw-filled pillow, with a pillowcase and a linen bag 5ft by 3ft that served as a sleeping bag, both of which were exchanged every month, and a blanket that was never exchanged and soon filthy. The rest of the furniture in the room was spartan with one cupboard between four, about seventy wooden stools and a dozen small tables, around each of which up to six could sit if the weather was poor and being outside did not appeal; those unable to find a seat could only stand or retire to their beds. In each room there was a small stove for which a very limited supply of coal was issued from mid-October through to March, but it did little to heat the room as they were to discover; at around 1,400ft above sea level as they were, the temperature hovered around or below freezing until late spring. Surviving on an inadequate amount of food and with most lacking any form of warm clothing, they felt the cold at night even in the summer months.

In the following days the new arrivals explored their home. Oflag VII-C, they discovered, consisted of two blocks connected by a lower, long narrow building with some 1,200 officers split between the two blocks, while the connecting building provided accommodation for the doctors and padres. Around 200 orderlies lived separately in a former stable block away from the main buildings beyond, which was an open area known as 'the park', a grandiose title for a sparsely grassed area about 70 yards square with one large tree in the middle and a path flanked by a 9ft high barbed wire fence, the whole dominated by a sentry tower and several sentry boxes. On the western side, beyond the wire a 10ft high wooden fence hid the main Laufen to Salzburg road from view, while to the south an orchard and the River Salsach lay beyond the wire. It was considered a very difficult camp from which to escape with the inherent problems of the location compounded by Oberst Frey appointing one of his officers with the specific role of preventing escapes. For the POWs, tunnelling appeared to be the only feasible option, albeit difficult, with foundations on one side of their prison and a drop to the river on the other limiting their choices of where to start a dig, the direction to take and the area to target for their exit.

Within the castle, washing facilities were adequate for 600, but when numbers rose to 1,200 the overcrowding became a problem, only partly relieved when a new camp designated Oflag VII-C/Z was opened in Tittmoning, 12 miles away to the north. Some 24 officers, including General Fortune and nine orderlies, were sent there on 30 August 1940, followed shortly after by a further 180 officers and 30 orderlies. Tittmoning was very different from Laufen in many ways; the prisoners were treated correctly, given decent shelter and food and allowed to receive Red Cross parcels, although they suspected the Germans sometimes kept a few back for themselves using as an excuse that deliveries had been held up by Allied air raids. The camp was established in a medieval fortress where many Channel Islanders and some Poles were already interned and was considered by the Germans as 'escape proof'; trying to disprove this was both a challenge and full-time sport to the imprisoned officers. However, their guards having already had the benefit of guarding enterprising Polish officers in the fortress always got the better of them, and although there were numerous attempts none resulted in a 'home run'. Standing instructions to guards from the Commandant of Tittmoning, Major von Spruner, made it clear that prisoners should not be treated unreasonably after escape attempts, pointing out that it was the officers' duty to attempt to escape and the guards should expect them to carry on trying. Several of the attempted ways to escape were to be repeated in later years, notably – and the method employed by Mike, Ronnie and Gris to escape from Posen – being concealed under piles of rubbish in a cart and wheeled out of the camp. There may not have been any 'home runs' made from Tittmoning, but the experience gained by the prisoners in their escape attempts was to prove invaluable to later plans.

In Laufen food, or the lack of it, preoccupied the minds of the officers. The rations supplied by the Germans were handed over to the British cookhouse staff who made themselves responsible for the cooking and distribution of the food. They did their best but it was soon apparent that the already skimpy rations allocated to the POWs were being pilfered by the camp authorities; following an investigation the British Quartermaster accused one of the German orderlies of theft, who promptly complained to his chain of command. The Commandant was incensed by the accusation and summoned the Quartermaster who was given a severe dressing down and threatened with solitary confinement for 'conduct unbecoming towards a member of the German armed forces'. The meagre amount of margarine the prisoners received was cut as both a punishment and a warning that such accusations would not be tolerated.

The rations issued to the officers in their first three months in Laufen, before a few personal and Red Cross parcels began to arrive in September, were limited in both variety and quantity, but nevertheless meals provided the high points of the daily routine to the hungry prisoners:

> 7 am, Individuals began to get up but it was possible to sleep on if you wished.
>
> 7.15 am, Room Duty Officer went to the kitchen to draw a jug of ersatz coffee. Others in the room would get up to wash and shave in one of the two washrooms available; there was usually a five-minute wait for one of the sixty to seventy basins in each washroom. Three or four individuals shared a mirror; razor blades were scarce, toothpaste rarely attainable and towel strips 2ft by 6in had to last a month. Some individuals dozed on until around 8 am before getting up to wash and shave.

By 7.30 am had drunk their coffee and perhaps breakfasted on a slice of their bread ration depending on how they preferred to eke it out, some ate a slice at lunch and tea with two at supper, others ate a day's or even a week's ration at a time and then went without. How to manage the bread ration provided a topic for endless discussion and debate.

8.45 am Morning roll call took place, the officers drawn up in blocks on a rank basis. The parade lasted for around 45 minutes depending on the competence of the guards and in later days, when they had regained some strength, how cooperative and compliant the officers were. After being fallen out, many headed to the canteen as soon as it opened at 9.30 am and, although designed to hold 80 to a 100 but now crammed with 400 to 500, they remained there for the rest of the morning. Others attended lectures from fellow prisoners on topics ranging from the art of wine-making to ancient Greek history, some retired to their beds to doze and smoke in solitude, a few would head to the exercise area and struggle around the 200-yard circuit, sit around or lean against something, deep in thought. Outside, there was much to admire in the views of the Bavarian Alps and their surroundings, albeit that the beauty of the vista accentuated the harsh reality of their confinement.

11 am, Officers began queuing to collect their lunch and retire to their rooms to eat. From Monday to Saturday they received half a bowl of soup, sometimes with a small piece of meat in it, and two potatoes, unless the soup was 'potato soup', in which case no additional potatoes were available. They ate out of their bowls with unseemly haste, those unable to get a seat climbing onto their bunks, something Gris – with his wound still open – found very

difficult. With the canteen shut and nowhere else to spend the time, the afternoons dragged by dozing, often dreaming of food; card games were popular and numerous recitals took place on the one piano in the camp, enabling individuals to immerse themselves in music and for a few moments forget their circumstances. Amateur dramatics were soon being staged, the production of costumes for which provided valuable experience in making clothing for use in later escape attempts.

4 – 5 pm, from around this time, later in the summer months, officers queued for their evening meal, another bowl of soup and two potatoes that, like lunch, was taken to their rooms and quickly eaten; on Sundays they also received a spoonful of jam, a very small pat of margarine, enough to spread on two days' bread ration, and a small milk cheese. The total amount of food they received daily was pitifully small, leaving them ravenously hungry and scouring the small outside area they were permitted to access for anything edible; grass, dandelions and nettles were consumed, and occasionally rats if they could catch them.

7 – 7.30 pm Again sometimes later in the summer months, was the evening parade. Officers formed up as for the morning roll call and waited to be counted. In the winter months it could be bitterly cold and the officers would do little to delay, hinder or prolong the count, but even so it was seldom complete in less than thirty minutes. Periodically during these parades, the rooms were inspected and the duty officer in each, responsible for sweeping out and tidying up, was required to be present while a German NCO walked around checking the cleanliness. A patch of dust or a scrap of paper found on the floor had to be removed immediately to avoid being

> reported as 'insolent' to the Commandant, inevitably found guilty and placed in solitary confinement for a number of days, living on bread and water, sleeping on bare boards, not being allowed to shave or read, and getting only thirty minutes exercise a day.
>
> Once evening roll call was over officers returned to their rooms and those who had kept some of their bread ration back had a slice for supper. In winter months if they were able somehow to 'acquire' a raw potato it was thinly sliced and stuck on the outside of the room stove to cook; they were ready once they fell off and made a welcome bit of variety in their monotonous diet.

Stomach upsets became prevalent at one time when the daily ration of potatoes was half-rotten but, being as short of food as they were, consumed nevertheless. Long queues formed at the lavatories and those 'caught short' were frequently unable to hold out until their turn so the area of the latrines soon became an unpleasant and unsanitary mess. In an effort to improve the health of the prisoners the Germans provided, on payment in camp money, a daily mug of separated milk; enterprising officers soon discovered that it could be turned into something akin to cottage cheese if tied up in an old sock and hung from the side of their bunk for a while.

Alongside the continuous hunger and quest for food, the lack of tobacco was a constant agony that had to be endured. Most young people at the time were habitual smokers and the ration of eight cigarettes every four days that the officers received was woefully short of being able to satisfy their craving; their choices ranged from smoking the eight cigarettes immediately, or two a day, or none until day four when they would smoke them all. Polish pipe tobacco was occasionally on sale in the canteen, but even for the heaviest smokers it was unpleasantly stringent. An enterprising Royal Marine officer tried blending it with dried droppings from the horses that pulled vegetable carts into the camp and offered his product to a pipe-smoking major as a better quality tobacco obtained from one of the guards. This 'tobacco' was duly swapped for a week's margarine ration and pronounced to be excellent by the major, who sought out his benefactor later to ask if more could be obtained.

Mike, Phil and Gris, with others from 2 KRRC, stuck together and had periodic dinners when each brought his own food and shared everything they had received in food parcels. For many months, conversation on these occasions revolved around menus and restaurants rather than escape. Lack of food made physical activity, even if not strenuous or demanding, difficult to sustain and the demands of being 'on the run' beyond their capabilities. Those who lived on the upper storey of their prison often found they were unable to walk up the three flights of stairs to reach their rooms without pausing for a few minutes on the way to avoid blacking out. All the prisoners lost weight and their physical weakness was extreme, but the notion of escape remained and as conditions slowly began to improve came increasingly to the forefront of their minds. Teasing the guards was an enjoyable diversion; in later years Lieutenant Colonel Ellison-Macartney of the QVR recalled the fun of teaching them colloquial English, causing on one occasion an enraged sergeant to shout out: 'You English think I know f**k nothing about your escape plans! Indeed, I know f**k all!'

To counter attempts to escape, the Germans set up a security staff controlled by an officer fluent in English assisted by a number of English-speaking NCOs. He was responsible for the layout of sentry posts and beats, barbed-wire placement and physical checks on the gates giving access to the camp; his staff were continuously on the lookout for signs and sounds of tunnelling, such as loose floorboards, noises from underground and the presence of obvious lookouts, as well as excavated spoil. He was good at his job and master of the situation; only one tunnel was completed successfully, enabling a party of six to get away in early September 1941, all were recaptured within days, returned to Laufen and given varying lengths of solitary confinement; before their sentences were complete these escapees were transferred to another camp Oflag IV-C, Colditz Castle; among them Major Pat Reid, whose experience would be put to good use in this new 'escape-proof' camp.[2]

Earlier, in 1941 there had been a tragic shooting incident in Laufen when Lieutenant Dees, 6 DLI, was killed by a German sentry. Dees was sketching from a third storey window in the centre of the building about 80 yards from the camp perimeter fence and the nearest sentry post, from which the guard on duty was observing him; Dees was resting his sketch pad on the window sill but not leaning out of the open window. The sentry was seen to shout and gesticulate, but Dees neither heard nor noticed him or his fellow officers in the exercise area who tried to alert him and he continued to sketch. Getting no response to his shouted warnings the sentry knelt down, took aim, and fired, hitting Dees in the head and tragically killing him. Following the incident Brigadier Nicholson demanded that the order not to lean out of windows be cancelled, or if not cancelled that enforcement should be other than by the use of firearms. This was refused by Oberst Frey, despite being supported by his Officers and NCOs on the guard force, and two further instances occurred when shots were fired at officers close to open windows and deemed by guards to be leaning out.

Following the successful September escape further ideas for tunnelling out of Laufen were developed and submitted to the SBO for approval by the Escape Committee, who exercised control of all plans to avoid clashes or activities that might compromise other escape efforts already underway. Authority had been given for a tunnel that was being planned with three teams to work on it; Ronnie Littledale asked Mike and Gris to join him and form one of these teams. It was a major dig that started in a small music room off the main recreation and canteen area which, being the only reasonably comfortable place in the camp, was always very crowded. The entrance to the tunnel had been carefully hidden to blend into the music room floor; once the wooden cover was in place and dust spread over the area it was only those 'in the know' who could locate it easily, to the casual visitor there was nothing in the room to indicate any activity underway beneath their feet. When the team was on construction duty it was Ronnie and Mike who went down the tunnel to dig, and Gris who stayed above ground taking up a position from where he could see through a peephole across the recreation area to the gallery on the far side, where a fourth person was positioned ready to alert him by hand signal if any Germans were approaching and about to cross the small yard leading to the recreation room. The tunnel was lit by a light bulb plugged into an adjacent wall socket and dangling into the tunnel shaft; on receiving a signal the electric wire would be pulled from the wall socket plunging the diggers below into darkness and alerting them to keep quiet.

On the third day of their tunnelling-duty spell, Gris received the 'Germans approaching' signal and pulled the wire out of the socket; below him Mike, who was digging, and Ronnie, who was removing the soil, suddenly in darkness, swiftly pulled in the wire, stayed still and quiet. Gris had just enough time to replace the tunnel cover, scuff the surrounding dust and sit down at the piano to play a few chords before three German soldiers burst in with a large Alsatian dog; Gris was ordered to stand up with his hands above his head while the Germans banged about on the floor until they found the tunnel cover. Once the lid was removed Gris was marched off to wait in the corridor outside the Commandants office. At the entrance to the tunnel Mike was soon pulled out covered in dust and dirt and marched off to join Gris, but despite their best efforts the Germans could not persuade their dog to go down into the tunnel and Ronnie was able to stay hidden, emerging later to slip away unnoticed. It would not be the only time Ronnie was able to remain hidden during an escape attempt while Mike, his fellow escapee, was spotted and captured.

Mike and Gris, having refused to answer any questions, were sentenced to forty-two days 'streng arrest' in solitary confinement in a cell block outside the camp. 'Streng Arrest' meant that the prisoner, entirely contrary to the Geneva Convention, was allowed no books, no writing materials, no cigarettes or tobacco, no cards, and for three days out of four slept on bare boards: on the fourth day the prisoner was allowed a mattress and got two meals of soup. Having nothing to do all day except pace your cell or sit and think was not a pleasant experience for those in solitary; Gris passed the time by reciting to himself the store of poems he had learned at school; there is no account of how Mike occupied his time, but given his dedication to escaping he almost certainly mulled over many ideas. The tedium of their solitary confinement was alleviated only by a daily walk in the camp exercise area where friends used to hide small packets of biscuits or other goodies that they were usually able to find under the snow now laying thickly on the ground.

Before their sentence was completed Mike and Gris were released back into the camp to prepare for a move to what they were told was a special camp called Fort VIII in Posen, a small town in Poland. After their time in Laufen it was both exciting and exhilarating to say goodbye to Oflag VII-C and be on the move once again. In later life Phil recalled the happier side of his time in Laufen; receiving his first letter from home, the first food and clothing parcels, ice skating on the rink the prisoners created by flooding an area of 'the park', and raucous parties when wine and beer flowed, special occasions that all shared and remembered. Fort VIII in Posen was not destined to hold such pleasant memories.

CHAPTER 5

FORT VIII – POSEN

In the second week in March 1941 five hundred selected officer POWs in Laufen were paraded very early one morning before being marched the short distance to the railway station and entrained for their journey to Posen

Posen, lying roughly midway between Warsaw and Berlin astride the direct route from Moscow to the German capital, was recognised as a key strategic defensive location and developed as such under Prussian rule in the nineteenth century with outer and inner rings of fortresses, but by the early twentieth century developments in artillery and munitions had made these defences largely ineffective; as a consequence they were no longer maintained and some, left unattended, were used for storage, or even housing, by the local population. In 1939, following the German invasion and occupation of Poland, a number of them were used to hold prisoners captured during the campaign; collectively they formed Stalag XXI-D. Fort VIII at Posen was one of them.

For the selected officers the prospect of being on the move to somewhere new was both exhilarating and exciting, and to their relief it was to be Third Class carriages rather than cattle trucks for this trip. Some, seeing it as an escape opportunity, began to make plans. Phil Pardoe and three others gathered what food and maps they could and managed to acquire the blade of a saw with the intention of cutting through the railway carriage floorboards. The 500 prisoners selected to be moved were paraded early one morning in the second week of March, and marched to the same railway station where they had disembarked many months before on arrival from Mainz. Despite the best efforts of the guards to keep the officers in their preordained groups, the march quickly degenerated into a disorderly straggle, enabling Phil and the others to stay together and get into the same Third Class compartment. Once locked in and underway they began to work on the floor of the compartment but quickly appreciated that cutting through it was impracticable and opted instead to split into two groups and jump from the train, one pair at a time, on consecutive days. However, the opportunity never arose and the journey, memorable for the cold, lack of water and discomfort, drew to a close three days later on arrival at Posen. Ronnie, Gris and Mike in a separate carriage had had the same idea of breaking through the carriage floor but constant interruptions at the appearance of guards in the corridor made the task too difficult and they too abandoned the attempt.

The POWs disembarked from their train on arrival at the station in Posen and were formed up with a lot of shouting from German police and military guards, some of the former mounted. It was a motley collection of individuals that set off on the two-to-three mile march to their new camp. There had been so little water available on the journey that no more than half a mug could be spared by the prisoners for washing and shaving. The best that could be achieved with such limited resources was a 'shaving brush wash', a system of covering the body with lather using a shaving brush and then wiping oneself dry with a towel. Their clothes were patched and darned, just holding together, and many wore brilliant blue greatcoats issued by the Germans that sported enormous gold chevrons. A few tin helmets were still in evidence, but most were hatless, and all were carrying bundles containing their carefully accumulated worldly possessions wrapped up in whatever they had managed to get their hands on. These were heavy loads for individuals in poor physical shape and progress was slow, despite the efforts of the Germans to chivvy them along; many of the marching prisoners were physically exhausted by the time they reached the forbidding entrance to Fort VIII and were halted in the moat. Here they waited for some time before being addressed by the Commandant, Major Muller, who told them through an interpreter that their presence in the fort was in response to the treatment meted out to German officers in Canada. He explained that in their capacity as the 'Protecting Power' for Germany, Swedish officials had visited a group of German prisoners who had just arrived in Canada and were accommodated in Fort Henry, Ontario, an early nineteenth-century fortification built to guard the outlet to the St Lawrence River and the Kingston Navy Yards during the American War of Independence. This fort was above ground, but in other respects not dissimilar in design to Fort VIII at Posen, and among the first sites that had been chosen as prison camps in the early years of the war; unfortunately, the Swedish delegation had not understood that it was only a holding camp pending the POWs' onward move to one of the permanent camps established elsewhere in the country. Having failed to question why conditions were so poor, the report submitted on their visit drew attention to 'the unacceptable conditions in which German prisoners of war are being held in Canada', prompting immediate outrage in Germany.

Major Muller went on to explain that as German officers in Canada were suffering unpleasant and undignified conditions, and since protests had not resulted in any change or improvement, the German Reich had decided that British officers would have to be treated in the same manner; Fort VIII had been chosen as appropriate for this purpose but it was an 'equality', not a 'reprisal', camp and as soon as conditions for the German officers improved so would those of the British officers. He then announced that each officer would be given an extra card to write home to inform their families of the conditions in which they were now living, and why; most of the cards were promptly torn up or completed with somewhat over enthusiastic details of their new home.

Once Major Muller had finished this 'welcome address' the officers were divided into groups of twenty and marched off through the gate of the fort to their new underground accommodation. As they descended into the gloomy, fetid corridors dripping with water, down a dark spiral staircase and into low vaulted rooms they began to appreciate that in many ways Laufen had been luxurious. Each room was lit by a single dim lightbulb and had a small, barred window looking out into the surrounding ditch. There was no furniture, no lockers, chairs or tables, and only two wooden platforms for sleeping space that ran the length of the room on both sides, 6ft 6in deep and allowing around 18in per man when they lay down. Bedding was issued but was damp and minimal, a single blanket and a 4ft square half blanket with a palliasse and pillow, both stuffed with wood shavings. An exploration of their new 'home', when the opportunity presented itself, gave the prisoners an idea of the layout of the two-storey brick-built fort they were now in, only the roof of which was visible above ground. They found they were housed on the upper gallery with all possible points of access to the outside securely barred, and from which a spiral staircase led to a lower level and gallery. In the centre of this lower gallery were the kitchens and at each end a pump from which all water for washing and cooking was drawn; the temperature of the water never varied from just above freezing.

The lavatories available were primitive and reminiscent of medieval 'privies' often found in castles, but the periodic cleaning out of the excrement that was necessary to keep them sanitary was clearly not happening. Holes had been cut in wooden planks laid over a hollow section of the fort outer wall above a sump that had long ago filled up and now overflowed into the surrounding area, a section of which, including the sump, had been wired off and designated as an exercise ground. The smell and flies around this sump were beyond description but even worse were the 'crabs', pubic lice, which infested the latrines and quickly spread to the newly arrived prisoners. An earlier inmate of Fort VIII had written on the wall: *'Be careful sitting on this seat for Posen crabs can jump ten feet.'*

The prisoners organised a competition to see who could catch the most lice from their blankets and clothes at bedtime; the method used was to run a piece of wet soap along the seams and count up the number that were collected on it. The record was 150.

Despite the damp, the fleas, their underground existence, the overflowing latrines and being locked in their rooms at night with a single bucket between the twenty or thirty in each room for any call of nature, it was a change of scene and welcomed by many if not all. Phil Pardoe was among the latter:

> The days seemed black indeed. So overcrowded that many of us had to share a bed, bitten by fleas and lice until people had septic legs, unable to read except on the window sill, mosquitoes rising from the overflowing sewers – the accumulation of horrors seemed at times unbearable.

Major General Victor Fortune, the most senior British officer in captivity, was also in Fort VIII. He had commanded 51st Division Highland Division assigned to French X Corps and remained in France after the evacuation from Dunkirk. Forced to surrender to avoid further casualties when naval evacuation proved impossible and supplies of ammunition and his troops were exhausted, 10 000d of his Division were taken prisoner at St Valery-en-Caux. Most were to spend four years in captivity during which Lieutenant Jimmy Atkinson of the 7th Battalion, Argyll and Sutherland Highlanders, composed 'The 51st Country Dance (Laufen Reel)', now better known as the Reel of the 51st. Given the circumstances it was originally an all-male Reel that was performed for the first time before Major General Fortune in Oflag VII-C, Laufen. Major General Fortune, who had elected to share the disagreeable conditions in Posen rather than be sent to a more comfortable camp for senior officers, tried hard to get conditions improved; he spoke no German but usually got what he wanted by speaking forcefully in English and was always supported by Colonel Willy Tod, Royal Scots Fusiliers, the designated Senior British Officer (SBO) in Posen and later to be the SBO in Colditz during a number of Mike's escape attempts. After several weeks Major General Fortune succeeded in getting the latrine sump emptied, a small but significant improvement in the conditions and lives of the prisoners that raised the morale and self-respect of all. He shared the privations of the underground life in Fort VIII and set a wonderfully cheerful example to all the officers. Gris remembered one typical example:

> On one occasion I was sitting on the loo in our very basic and substandard lavatory when the General went into the next compartment. After a short time he suddenly said: 'I say you next door, do you think there are as many flies in your pan as there are in mine?'

Once they had settled in the officers began to scour the fort for anything they could find to improve their lives; the occasional pieces of wood they discovered were quickly turned into rough furniture making a significant difference to their comfort in what were appalling conditions. The general atmosphere was damp and dingy with rats scuttling about, but thankfully not in large numbers, unlike the fleas and lice that plagued the rooms and seemed to thrive on the flea powder that the Germans, acknowledging the problem, allowed the prisoners to buy. Despite the conditions the prisoners remained surprisingly healthy, mild dysentery and foot rot (similar to athletes foot) being the most prevalent complaints. Somewhat surprisingly, most found Fort VIII an improvement over Laufen and had no desire to return there.

Three weeks after their move to Posen, Mike and Gris were summoned to appear before the Commandant and were locked up together in a turret to complete the remaining ten days of their Laufen sentence, but without the 'bread and water' diet and with beds in place of bare boards for sleeping. These improvements were offset, however, by the presence of rats behind the wooden panelling on the lower part of the walls; when they first entered the room, they found one, more curious or bold than the rest, sitting on one of the beds waiting to greet them. After pointing this out to the guard and complaining forcefully, a hammer, nails and length of tin sheeting were provided enabling them to seal off the skirting; although the rats were still noisy at night, they were no longer able to get into the room, despite their efforts to gnaw a way through the tin. Contrary to their previous experiences the guards were content to allow Mike and Gris access to an outside tap each evening to wash and although the water was cold, they used to spin out their ablutions by stripping off for an all over wash – much to the guards' surprise and concern for their wellbeing. Although their period of confinement passed relatively quickly and was much less unpleasant than their experience in Laufen, they were glad nevertheless to put it behind them.

Some weeks later, around May 1941, there was a sudden and unexpected improvement in the conditions at Fort VIII. In January of that year Hauptman Franz von Werra, a Luftwaffe officer, who had been shot down in September 1940 and sent to Canada with other POWs, had managed to escape. After successfully crossing the frozen St Lawrence River he had entered the USA making his way to New York and thence Mexico, finally reaching Germany via South America, Spain and Italy nearly eight months later on 18 April 1941. On his return Werra reported to the German High Command on his treatment while in Canada as a POW and was sent to Fort VIII to see how accurately the conditions there replicated those he had experienced as recorded by the Swedish Delegation after their visit to Fort Henry. After looking around he asked for how long the British officers were held in these conditions and was horrified on being told 'until such time as the reported treatment of German officers [in Fort Henry] is improved'; he was able to explain that Fort Henry was a transit camp and that German officers spent, at most, no more than a couple of days there before being moved on to a permanent camp. On hearing this Major Muller acted immediately, assembling the POWs to explain the misunderstood Swiss Delegation report that had caused their transfer to Posen and the conditions imposed on them there. He apologised for the misunderstanding and, acknowledging that it would be some time before they could be moved elsewhere, did what he could to improve the situation by allowing them access to the roof of the fort during daylight hours.

Soon after these welcome relaxations Red Cross parcels began to arrive weekly and were shared out among the officers, making a significant improvement to their well-being. The contents varied in these early days of the war, often depending on the country of origin, but a typical parcel would contain small tins of meat (spam or corned beef) or alternatively fish (salmon or herring), small portions of jam, perhaps Marmite if the parcel came from Britain, powdered milk, powdered eggs, cheese, raisins, tea, biscuits and sweets, frequently in the form of a small 2oz chocolate bar, and – most important for many – cigarettes. To the prisoners these were luxuries indeed; chocolate, as had happened earlier with cigarettes, became a 'currency' and could be bartered for other commodities, while the packaging from the parcels was equally useful as the prisoners sought to make themselves more comfortable. Nothing was discarded, the string which tied the parcels together was turned into shoes, bags, brushes and hammocks, and the tins kept for brewing tea and coffee. Later, in Colditz, as they became more organised and their escape attempts more sophisticated, German uniform insignia and accoutrements were fashioned using tin and cardboard from the Red Cross parcels they received.

There were other improvements to the officers' living conditions; tables, stools, lockers and two-tier iron beds appeared in the rooms, the lighting was improved and Major General Fortune was given a room for himself and his ADC. A plot of ground outside the fort was provided for use as a garden and a number of officers were allowed out daily to tend it, but two of the biggest causes for complaint, the lack of showers and delay in receiving mail, remained unresolved. As conditions improved, and with the coming of spring, thoughts turned back to escape from what, of necessity up until then, had been the daily concentration on surviving the miseries of their underground confinement. It soon became apparent that without some coordination, escape plans could clash and well thought through efforts be scuppered by more amateur efforts easily detected and thwarted by the German guard force. To separate and prioritise escape plans Colonel Tod, acting in his designated role of SBO and assisted by Captain Ross of the Cameron Highlanders as his deputy, set up an Escape Committee, to whom those with a plan presented their idea for consideration. If necessary, the plan could then be coordinated with other proposals and given a priority. With the blessing of the Escape Committee Ronnie, Mike and Gris began work on a trapdoor covering for the entrance to a tunnel they planned to dig under the moat with help from Phil, Peter Douglas[1] and Philip Taylor. After weeks of work the trap door was complete, camouflaged and in place, but as soon the team started digging and removing earth water began to flow into the hole they created. Tunnelling there was obviously not going to be possible and reluctantly they abandoned the idea.

Not long after giving up this attempt the Germans discovered the abandoned tunnel entrance and an amused Major Muller mocked their efforts, suggesting that those digging 'should have sought his advice about the water table'. He went on to assure them that it was not possible to get out of the fort – and even if they did by some chance manage to escape, open country surrounded them and beyond that Russia, 'where they would likely be shot on arrival', or the Baltic ports that were 'too closely guarded to offer a chance of boarding a vessel bound for Sweden or elsewhere', while the idea of reaching

Switzerland 600 miles away was 'fanciful'. So certain was he of the impossibility of escape that he allowed the POWs a considerable amount of freedom and even provided tools so that they could tend their garden plots outside the fort; the 2 KRRC officers, although disappointed that their efforts had come to nothing, continued to look for opportunities to break out. Exploring the fort, they discovered a room on the far side of the moat which they believed would be suitable as a start point for a tunnel, only to be disappointed again when another group, who had also noted the possibility, submitted a plan ahead of them that was approved by the Escape Committee. That group broke out successfully through the tunnel they dug but were recaptured within days and returned to Fort VIII for a spell of solitary confinement, not a severe or particularly unpleasant experience since they were locked up as a group and found it was a simple job to pick the lock, let themselves out and return when the guards did their rounds.

Thoughts of escape and the search for how to get out of the fort were constantly on the minds of many of the prisoners and as spring arrived warmer weather and lighter evenings made confinement ever more irksome. Walks on the roof of the fort were authorised, and extended hours meant the prisoners could spend most of the daylight hours there if they wished, but they were always rounded up and returned below ground behind locked doors well before sundown. Watching from the roof enabled the prisoners to identify and note the daily routine followed by the British orderlies in disposing of rubbish from the cookhouse. Garbage was put into sacks that were then placed in a handcart; when full, usually two or three times a day, the cart was collected by the orderlies and carried by them over the moat to the main gate. The orderlies shouted to attract the attention of the guard commander who then unlocked the gate and supervised by a member of the guard, the orderlies wheeled the cart to the rubbish pit about 80 yards away, emptied the sacks into it and returned to camp. This routine disposal of the garbage offered distinct possibilities for getting out of the fort but required the acquiescence of the two orderlies, who would be disposing of the rubbish and somehow finding a reliable contact on the outside to help the onward journey once out.

It was Mike who studied the routine over many days and devised a plan that was submitted to the Escape Committee and approved. Given this authority to go ahead he befriended a young Polish boy who was working with a German electrician in the camp on a daily basis and through him was able to make contact with the Polish Resistance movement in Posen. The last piece in the escape plan was now in place and intense preparations began to acquire a map and compass, washing and shaving kit to ensure they could maintain a respectable appearance and, most difficult of all, German currency. Finding civilian-type clothing proved to be a serious problem, none was available from among the POWs so the only solution was to manufacture items from blankets and any scraps of material that were available. How to smuggle themselves out of the camp in the garbage sacks was practised and it was soon clear that the handcarts were too small, they needed to be large enough to carry one of them, but not so much bigger that it was noticeable. Making a slightly larger cart that would not attract attention, was strong enough for the task and could still be handled by the orderlies was the solution on which surreptitious work began.

When preparations were complete the countdown to the date chosen for the attempt began; it was to be 28 May 1941 – almost exactly a year since the fall of Calais and their capture. For all those involved in supporting them, and for the escape party in particular, this was an exciting if nerve-wracking time. Pat Reid, who made a 'home run' later from Colditz, summarised it succinctly:

> 'I can think of no sport that is the peer of escape where freedom, life and loved ones are the prize of victory and death the possible, though by no means inevitable, price of failure.'

The plan was for Mike to go first and once dumped in the rubbish pit, to climb out of the sack that had hidden him, wriggle to a spot from where he could see the roof of the fort and await the signal that it was safe to emerge. On receiving it he would climb out of the pit, make his way into the town and contact the Polish underground; using the same technique Ronnie and Gris would follow as the opportunity arose. On the morning of the 28th, they put on their carefully made civilian clothes; Mike wore an old French army coat which he had altered and succeeded in dyeing. It had taken a lot of experimentation to create an effective and lasting black dye before it was discovered that soaking the coarse black Polish tobacco, obtainable in the canteen, to make it palatable turned the water black; boiling packets of the tobacco in water produced a black, thick and sticky liquid that made a satisfactory and lasting dark blue/black dye. Gris used it on a pair of trousers and a civilian shirt, and Mike had a Dutch overcoat and pair of trousers both dyed black; Ronnie had obtained an old mackintosh and a pair of flannel trousers. Mike and Ronnie wore civilian caps and carried compasses that they had acquired, along with 180 Reich Mark to share between all three of them.[2] Thus dressed and prepared they settled down to await the arrival on duty of the particular guard they had identified over prolonged observation as 'somewhat lazy', since he did not follow the orderlies right up to the pit to see the rubbish unloaded, but watched from the path about 10 yards away as the carts were emptied and the rubbish sacks dumped into the pit.

CHAPTER 6

STEPS TO FREEDOM

Successful escape from Posen was the start of a long period 'on the run' in occupied Europe for Ronnie Littledale, Mike Sinclair and Gris Davies-Scourfield. All were destined to be recaptured and sent to Colditz Castle, the prisoner of war camp that had been established for 'persistent escapers'.

At around 10.30 am it was confirmed by the 'stooges' (the nickname given to those fellow prisoners who assisted in the act of escaping by secretly monitoring and reporting the movements of the German guard force), that the guard they were patiently awaiting was on duty, triggering their carefully formulated and rehearsed plan of escape from Fort VIII. Mike was helped into a rubbish sack and loaded into the adapted cart for the short move to the rubbish pit; watched surreptitiously from the roof of the fort by fellow prisoners, their meticulously planned routine was seen to work smoothly, the contents of the cart were dumped into the pit without incident and the orderlies returned to the fort. Climbing out from his sack Mike wriggled to a position that allowed him to see the roof of the fort and awaited the 'all clear' signal. It was not long coming and after clambering out of the pit, and without glancing back, he set off to walk into the town. It was a great moment for all involved in the plan, and especially for the orderlies who had managed to carry the heavily laden cart without arousing suspicion.

All was going to plan until midday, when the Commandant unexpectedly ordered a parade of the orderlies for 3 pm, meaning that Ronnie and Gris had to be moved out and 'dumped' in the rubbish pit earlier than intended. Ronnie was first to go and once the orderlies were back in the fort and the all clear signal was given he was quickly out onto the road and away. Time was short so Gris swiftly clambered into his sack in the cart and was covered up with rubbish:

> 'It all seemed to happen too quickly for me to have any last-minute nerves, although I was naturally keyed up to the limit. I was emptied out satisfactorily, my "all clear" signal was given – and away I went.'[1]

The enforced early start of their escape disrupted the agreed plan for meeting up with Mike at a tram terminus about three-quarters of a mile from Fort VIII and left them with over an hour to fill before their agreed rendezvous (RV). There was nothing to do except walk around the streets of Posen trying not to look conspicuous or attract attention, feeling all the time that they must look slightly strange and would arouse curiosity but it was exhilarating to be free and to have outwitted their German captors even if the ultimate goal of making it back to England was still a long way off. At 4 pm Gris made his way to the RV where Ronnie was already waiting, standing next to a tree and looking around nervously. As Gris approached, Ronnie gave him a quick look and crossed the road to avoid him; when Gris followed him Ronnie immediately crossed back over the road followed again by Gris who eventually caught up with him:

> 'Oh, it's you is it?' said Ronnie.
> 'Who on earth did you think it was?' replied Gris.
> 'Well, you look a bit different in those clothes and you've shaved off your moustache. I thought you were some inquisitive Pole trying to come and chat with me.'

The arrangement made with Mike was that the person coming to collect them would take off his hat and scratch his head, they would then do the same but by 4.15 pm despite scratching their heads on several occasions as people came past them, they had had no response. Mike had said that if they had had no success making contact by 4.30 pm, they should assume he had been caught and abandon the hope of getting help from any local Poles. If this happened their alternative plan was to secrete themselves aboard a goods train to Stuttgart that they knew was scheduled to leave at 9 pm that evening. The agreed time of 4.30 pm came with no contact made, but they decided to hang on for another fifteen minutes before switching to their alternative plan. Ten minutes later they recognised the young Polish electrician they had befriended walking towards them who, to their great relief, took off his cap and scratched his head.

The three of them walked together into the town and were taken into one of the flats in a block near the centre where they found Mike talking with two women. It was a joyful reunion that was celebrated with a tea such as they had not enjoyed since leaving England: white bread, butter, jam and cakes were produced and relished. A short while later they were split up and led away individually by guides to separate locations.

The place to which Gris was taken was typical, a two-room basement flat with a lavatory and kitchen that was home to a family with three children; they were extremely welcoming, though nervous at his presence, and eager to hear his thoughts on the war and how long it might last. There were many Germans in uniform around the town and the three escapees were moved separately to different locations each day for a number of days. Before the war 80 per cent of the population in Poland was Polish, but by the summer of 1941 this had been reduced to 15 per cent by mass arrests and deportations to. Western Poland had been taken into the 'Reich', while the centre of the country, including Warsaw and Cracow, had become part of the 'The General Government' surrounded by a controlled customs border, in effect a form of German colony. Eastern Poland had been annexed by Russia with the Poles who lived there, including women and children, being moved out – some on foot or transported, some in open trucks, but most by rail packed 150 or more into cattle wagons as the British POWs from Calais had experienced. With only the food and drink they had managed to carry with them, no sanitation and overcrowding, a number died on the journey with the bodies lying in the wagons until the doors were opened at their destination and the corpses thrown out. The living disembarked, often not knowing where they were in the 'General Government' area and were left without support to find their own shelter, food and if possible, work. Many thousands died.

In the vacated Polish neighbourhoods, the Nazis created enclaves, moving out any remaining ethnic or religious groups such as Christians, and replacing them with four times the number of Jews. Construction of walls or barbed wire barriers around these areas had begun in April 1940 and in October of that year the Nazis announced the building of 'residential quarters', soon called 'ghettos', within them. Before the war Warsaw had been a major centre of Jewish life and culture in Poland, and home to more than 350,000, about 30 per cent of the city's total population; it was the largest Jewish community in Europe and second in size only to New York City. Now these people were to be confined to an area of just over one and a third square miles. Those living in Warsaw, and those deported from other places throughout Western Europe, were ordered to move into the closed-off ghetto, where the entrance and external perimeter were guarded by German and Polish police and a Jewish militia had been formed to operate inside. Unemployment in the ghetto was a major problem so clandestine workshops were created and raw materials smuggled in to manufacture goods that could be sold, illegally, on the outside. Public soup kitchens were established to supplement the daily individual food ration provided by the authorities of 200 calories – well below the level needed to sustain good health in an adult. Orphanages, refugee centres and recreation facilities were formed, as well as schools – some of which operated under the guise of soup kitchens, but the Germans allowed only two hospitals for the growing numbers in the ghetto and requisitioned much of the medicines, instruments and equipment, including beds. Many within the ghetto died from starvation or mass epidemics such as typhoid and, as most could not afford the burial costs, the streets filled with corpses. By the summer of 1941 some 5–6,000 people were dying every day.

On their third day in Warsaw the three fugitives were taken individually to a large flat occupied by a woman in her mid-thirties and her small daughter. Mike made contact with some Poles who assured him they could provide clothing, papers and contacts further east, and that he and the others would be 'passed down the line' that had been established to assist escaped POWs reach friendly territory. The next day they were introduced to a distinguished looking elderly man who, they were told, should be referred to as 'The Doctor'; he spoke excellent English and without any hesitation or trace of self-importance, said it was fortunate he had come as he could, and would, help them. He then left, taking Mike with him to discuss what needed to be done while assuring Ronnie and Gris that he 'would be back later with Lieutenant Sinclair'. True to his word he returned with Mike, two other Poles and a bottle of brandy, to agree with them the plan that had been evolved and explain the next steps. The three escapees were to remain where they were for a few days while the plan was firmed up and contacts arranged along the route. Since a German woman living in the next flat shared the adjacent kitchen, they were to be hidden in a small box-room that had, they found, space for only one of them at a time to stand up and were not to leave the flat night or day. As soon as possible, accompanied by Nicholas, a young Pole who was hoping to reach England, they were to be moved on to Lodz by car where further arrangements for their journey would be made. They were destined to spend ten days confined to the box-room with occasional visits from the Doctor or Nicholas, who brought them news, and on one occasion a barber who bleached Gris' hair, eyebrows and moustache a golden copper colour, darkened down Mike's ginger hair and turned Ronnie's hair grey. On the ninth day of their incarceration the Doctor visited and told them to be ready to move at 9 am the following day; he would be standing across the street and when he removed his hat they were to leave the flat one by one with a short gap between each of them and get into the red car that would be at the corner. The driver, who was half German, had been told they were travelling to Lodz on business, and it was important he did not discover who they really were; Nicholas would converse with him but if he did try to speak to them, Mike would answer.

By 9.15 am the next morning they had been picked up and were in open country. Mike had ensured that the driver did not get curious at the silence of Ronnie and Gris by explaining they were suffering from nervous strain having been caught in a recent bombing raid on Hamburg. After a four-hour drive they left the taxi at the outskirts of Lodz and went on by tram through the Jewish ghetto, noticing the crowding and the yellow 'Star of David' that had to be worn by everyone, including children; it was the first evidence they had seen of the Nazi treatment of the Jewish people. They did not know it, but the ghetto they were travelling through was the second largest in the Reich and the most oppressively imposed. Some 164,000 Jews from Lodz were interned there with many thousands more, as well as Romas and Gypsies, gathered in from around the Reich. In January 1942, these numbers were reduced when deportations and mass executions commenced, but the mortality rate remained high with around 43,500 of those who were confined in the ghetto destined to die of cold, starvation and disease.

When the tram reached the centre of the town Mike, Ronnie and Gris left it and walked some distance to the address given to them by the Doctor. The inability to do much more than sit during their ten days confined to the box-room had left them weak, and the walk was certainly more an endurance march than a stroll for them. Their destination was a large, sparsely furnished flat where the owner, an elderly man by the name of Mr Wolf, was living with his nephew; both were pleased to see them and did not appear in the least concerned at giving them shelter. Shortly after their arrival Nicholas went out, returning with two young ladies from the local resistance who brought with them a deck of cards and some books and magazines to read, and who talked enthusiastically about crossing into 'The General Government' area, but were vague about how to do so and how to acquire the necessary ID cards. The following day Nicholas went out, returning shortly after with a tough-looking sailor who he introduced as a friend and with whom he went into the town each day thereafter to contact people who would be able to help them cross the border into the General Government. Mr Wolf and his nephew set off early each day for work, so Ronnie, Mike and Gris were free to discuss the situation and their options. They agreed that reaching Russia should be their goal; the annexation of eastern Poland had moved that frontier as far west as the river Bug, and made it easier to reach than the frontiers with Sweden, Turkey or Switzerland; they also talked over the risk their presence might pose to those Poles who were helping them so willingly, but despite their concerns concluded that the assistance they were receiving offered a real chance of success that they should not forego.

After ten days Gris was the first to be moved on; Nicholas collected him, took him by tram to a cafe in the north-eastern outskirts of the city and introduced him to a woman before leaving to return to the others; after hanging around until dusk Gris and his lady companion were picked up with others and taken east towards the border delineating the General Government area. As night fell their fellow travellers alighted at intervals until they were the only two left with the driver. After passing through a large wood they came to the outskirts of a village where they dismounted at the first cottage and said goodbye to the driver. The occupants of the cottage greeted them warmly and shared their food with them before they all settled down for the night to discover that the number of bugs and lice in the furniture made sleeping on the floor a better choice.

At first light Gris and his guide set out, glad to be away from the fleas and lice and grateful to have been spared their bites. They walked about two miles to another village and were welcomed into one of the first houses they reached to be given a very welcome breakfast that they shared with Ronnie and the 'sailor', who came in as they were sitting down. While they ate the positions and movements of the border guards were being monitored and relayed to their helpers; when an 'all clear' message came through Gris set off first with his guide. They were ignored by a German policeman that they passed, but hailed soon after by another who dismounted from his bicycle and came over. Instructions were whispered to Gris by the girl; 'look as stupid as you can and say nothing'. On being asked where they were going she explained that they were en route to visit a cousin for a short holiday and that Gris was her brother, but mentally handicapped; he assumed a suitably vague expression in support. After checking their bags, and admonishing them for having too much sugar and jam, the policeman accepted an invitation from the girl to 'drop into my cafe for a drink' and allowed them to go on their way while he peddled off. After a few hundred yards they went into another cottage where the girl took her leave and set off to return to Lodz.

Gris was in the cottage with the woman who lived there for three or more hours before the message came through that the border patrols had moved on. He was given some Polish money by the woman and told that it was now safe to cross the border marked by the railway line at the end of the road. Her daughter with the 'sailor' would lead the way; Ronnie and Gris were to keep 50 yards behind. When Ronnie appeared walking up the road Gris fell in alongside him and together, feeling very conspicuous, they reached the railway line and crossed it. They were now in the General Government of Poland and had left Germany.

CHAPTER 7

WARSAW SOJOURN

Entering the General Government area was another milestone on their journey and to be celebrated as a further step towards their goal of getting back to England and playing a part in the war. Ronnie and Gris walked on following their two guides, pausing after a few hundred yards to rid themselves of the forged identity papers they had been given in Warsaw. A short distance further on they were directed into a house with a room at the back where there were two beds; they slept well after a good meal prepared by the lady of the house from the food they had brought with them. When they woke in the morning 'the sailor' set off into the town ahead of them to find accommodation but returned having had no success. They could not stay where they were as the room was no longer available, so they bedded down for the night in a barn near the border crossing point they had used. Mike and Nicholas arrived in the morning, having crossed the border accompanied by the girl who had helped the others and, all together once again, they set off for the rendezvous they had been given in a café walking in groups spread out over several hundred yards. Feeling very conspicuous they entered the café where Mike, Ronnie and Gris sat down at a table, heads huddled together as if they were deep in a private conversation. Nicholas, 'the sailor' and the girl sitting together at a separate table learned the news of the German invasion of Russia, the consequences of which would necessitate a re-examination of their plan to seek a route home that way.

Their indecision and gloom was alleviated by 'the sailor' who had contacts in Tomaszow, a town about twenty-five miles away; the girl agreed to take a train there and arrange somewhere for them to stay while they walked there. It was a long and hot day as they followed tracks and lanes to their destination where they were met on arrival that evening and taken to a cottage. Tired and thirsty after their long trek, they were given a warm welcome and, most importantly, enjoyed a good meal after which the girl who had been their guide, and whose name they never knew, said her goodbyes and set off to return to Lodz. There was a barn at the back of the cottage where they settled down for the night and remained the next day while Nicholas and 'the sailor' went into the town, returning that evening downhearted with a newspaper carrying a report on '*Unternehmen Barbarossa'*, Operation Barbarossa, the German invasion of Russia, and confirming the full-scale retreat of the Russian forces opposing them *'vom Nordcap bis zum Schwarzen Meer'*. The implication of the newspaper article was that both the Finns in the north and Romanians in the south had allied themselves with Germany, and the rapid advance of their combined forces made the hope of reaching safety in Russia unlikely. To add to the gloom Nicholas and 'the sailor' had not found anyone willing to help them since the local police appeared to be aware that they were in the area and were inquiring if anyone had seen them.

It was clear that their plans had to be revised, if not completely scrapped, and they sat down in an orchard in the sunshine to consider what they should do. After discussing the options, they agreed that their initial feeling had been correct, and although the situation was unclear there was little hope now of finding safety in Russia as they had expected. Nicholas believed their best option was to return to Warsaw where he had contacts, and they could blend into the population safely while working out a new course of action. 'The sailor', however, had lost heart and decided to return to Posen, as in his view it was clearly no longer possible to reach safety in Russia;

Right: Mike Sinclair

Below: Improvised road block, Calais

Above: POW marched away from Calais

Below: Posen today

Above: Posen, 1942

Below: Mike and Gris circled

Above: Mike and Gris, Colditz

Below: Wanted Notice for Mike and Klein page 1

Deutsches Kriminalpolizeiblatt

(Sonderausgabe)

Herausgegeben vom Reichskriminalpolizeiamt in Berlin

Erscheint täglich mit Ausschluß der Sonn- und Feiertage | Zu beziehen durch die Geschäftsstelle Berlin C 2, Werderscher Markt 5—6

15. Jahrgang	Berlin, den 30. November 1942	Nummer 4447 a

Nur für deutsche Behörden bestimmt!

Entwichene kriegsgefangene Offiziere

A. Neuausschreibungen.

I. Aus dem Lager in Wahlstatt bei Liegnitz entwichener französischer Offizier.

(Nachtrag zu Sonderausgabe DtKPBl Nr. 4441 a I vom 23. 11. 42.)

Linossier, Henry, Oblts., 10. 7. 12 Fouillouse, Gef.-Nr. 449, ist noch nicht ergriffen. Er ist am Schluß dieser Nummer zu I abgebildet.

K III 64999/42. 27. 11. 42. **KPLSt Breslau.**

II. Aus dem Lager in Colditz i. Sa. entwichener französischer und englischer Offizier.

(Nachtrag zu DtKPBl Nr. 4446 a I vom 28. 11. 42.)

Klein, Charles, franz. Hauptmann, 29. 8. 10 Grenoble, Gef.-Nr. 260 VIII, und
Sinclair, Michael, brit. Ltn., 26. 2. 18 London, Gef.-Nr. 830 VII C,
sind noch nicht ergriffen. Sie sind am Schluß dieser Nummer zu II und III abgebildet.

6 K 34526/42. 28. 11. 42. **KPSt Leipzig.**

III. Aus der Haft in Meppen entwichene polnische Zivilarbeiter.

(Nachtrag zu DtKPBl Nr. 4446 a III vom 28. 11. 42.)

Otremba, Max, 23. 11. 13 Gay, Kr. Löbau (Westpr.), und Rzadkiewicz, Kasimir, 21. 1. 20 Smolary, Kr. Wongrowitz, | sind noch nicht ergriffen. Sie sind am Schluß dieser Nummer zu IV und V abgebildet.

II E 4042/42. 26. 11. 42. **Stapo Osnabrück.**

Die Flüchtigen sind festzunehmen und Grenzübertritte mit allen Mitteln zu verhindern.

Es sind die für diese Fälle vorgesehenen Fahndungsmaßnahmen einzuleiten.

Reichskriminalpolizeiamt — C —

Bildveröffentlichungen zur Nr. 4447 a d. Deutschen Kriminalpolizeiblattes

Above: Wanted Notice for Mike and Klein page 2

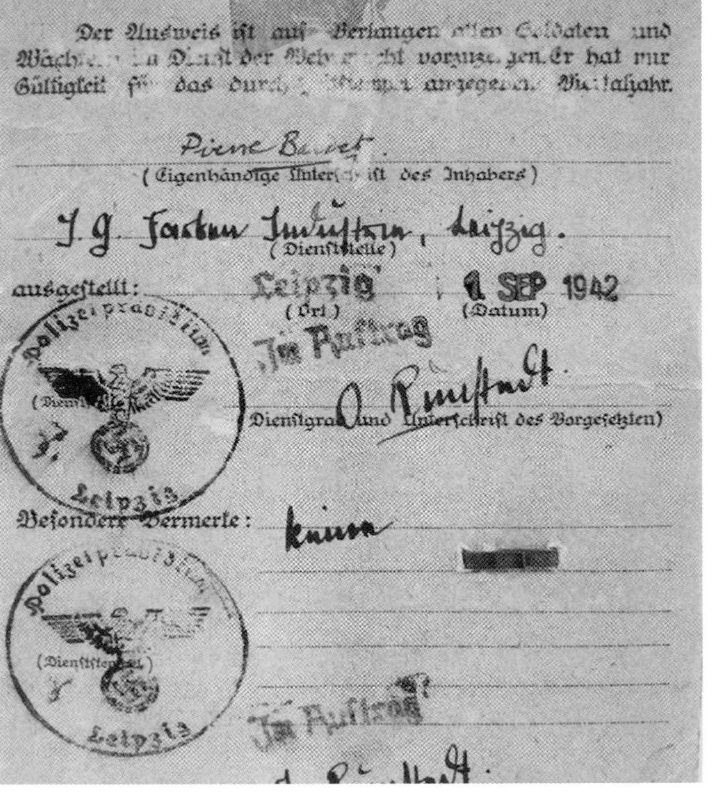

Der Ausweis ist auf Verlangen allen Soldaten und Wächtern im Dienst der Wehrmacht vorzuzeigen. Er hat nur Gültigkeit für das durch [illegible] angegebene Vierteljahr.

Pierre Bardet.
(Eigenhändige Unterschrift des Inhabers)

J. G. Farben Industrie, Leipzig.
(Dienststelle)

ausgestellt: Leipzig 1 SEP 1942
(Ort) (Datum)

Im Auftrag
[illegible]
(Dienstgrad und Unterschrift des Vorgesetzten)

Polizeipräsidium (Dienststelle) Leipzig

Besondere Vermerke: keine

Polizeipräsidium (Dienststelle) Leipzig

Im Auftrag

Right: Fake ID page 1

Fake ID page 2

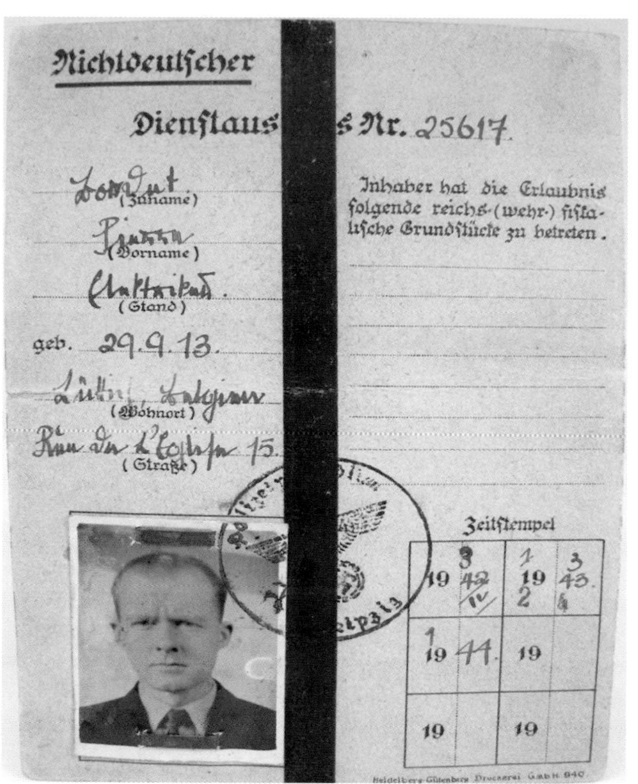

Nichtdeutscher

Dienstaus[weis] Nr. 25617.

(Zuname)

(Vorname)

(Stand)

geb. 29.9.13.

(Wohnort)

15.
(Straße)

Inhaber hat die Erlaubnis folgende reichs-(wehr-) fiskalische Grundstücke zu betreten.

Zeitstempel

Heidelberg-Gutenberg Druckerei G.m.b.H. 940

Colditz castle from the west

it was a blow as they had been relying on him increasingly since he had joined them. Psychologically for Mike, Ronnie and Gris, giving up was not an option and they were determined to go on together, but they needed help in obtaining the identity papers and travel documents without which they were likely to be picked up quickly. Nicholas gave them the address of a sweet shop on Chmielna Street in Warsaw where, he said, they would be collected and given the help they needed. Leaving 'the sailor' to return to Posen alone, Nicholas took a train to Warsaw to make the necessary arrangements for their return while Mike, Ronnie and Gris walked the seventy miles to the city.

Having agreed to retrace their steps they had supper and an early night, planning to set off at 3 am the next morning. They were up and away promptly on a cold, clear morning making their way through the village causing all the dogs to bark furiously but prompting no human interest. As the sun came up the temperature rose and they slaked their thirst from the occasional wells they passed, or by asking for water from cottages. Nobody seemed inquisitive about them and none of the German soldiers heading east in long streams of trucks, nor the occasional policeman they saw, took any notice of them. They took the precaution, nevertheless, of stopping for the night in the depths of a large wood – regretting the decision when evening fell and clouds of mosquitoes descended on them, making sleep impossible. As dawn broke, they moved back to the edge of the wood and watched a column of mounted cavalry riding towards Warsaw, but it was an hour before the road was clear and they were able to leave their hiding place to check a nearby signpost that showed they had walked forty-five kilometres the day before. It was another very hot day and they became increasingly thirsty walking through undulating countryside with the road still running, as far as they could tell, roughly north east. Most of the people they asked for water were friendly, but not inquisitive, and happy to give them a drink – although at one cottage Mike was bitten in the leg by a dog set on him by its unfriendly and suspicious owner. As night approached, they realised the open countryside gave them little opportunity of finding a secure place to bed down and so decided to go back to a wood they had passed two miles back.

Once they reached the wood they paused to have something to eat before going too far in, but a heated argument about water broke out. Ronnie said he needed to drink before he ate as his mouth was so dry; Gris believed they should eat first and drink later when they would be even more thirsty; Mike concluded the debate by saying he was not prepared to ask for water twice and they ate in tense silence before going to a cottage to ask for water. Having slaked their thirst, they worked their way into the depths of the wood and settled down for the night. It was a short time only before mosquitoes found them and quickly made any attempt to sleep impossible; Mike in particular seemed to be targeted, and before long insisted that they move out into the open in the hope that the mosquitoes would not follow them. They found a small hollow in the heath and settled again for the night but were quickly located by the mosquitoes in even greater numbers. While Ronnie and Gris were able to get some rest despite being bitten, Mike had a torrid time; his ginger hair and reddish skin seemed to attract the mosquitoes so rather than attempt to sleep he spent the night walking about and waving his arms around to try and beat them away. It was a relief to them all, but especially to Mike, when dawn came at 4 am and they were able to resume their walk to Warsaw now only 15-and-a-half miles away.

They plodded on hot, tired and increasingly thirsty, reaching the outskirts of the city sooner than they had expected but not risking a break as so many people were strolling about and they feared being drawn into conversation if they sat down to rest. The city stretched away before them in a seemingly endless succession of tower blocks as they walked and walked ever more slowly with Mike in particular somewhat short tempered and, after his sleepless night, finding it hard to keep up as they trudged along into the town. They were now only

25 kilometres from Warsaw but had the problem of finding Chmielna Street, their solution was to take a 'drozka', a horse drawn cab, that had the benefit of resting their weary legs. After passing through the battle-damaged city and reaching the railway station, they alighted and set off to find the sweet shop where they had been told they would be expected. But at the address they had been given, there was no shop selling sweets – only a café that would not open until 9 am. That left them with two hours to fill on the open streets, all while trying not to attract attention or arouse any suspicion that might lead to them being stopped, questioned, and discovered without identity papers. Although tired and thirsty they had no choice but to walk around the increasingly busy streets trying to act naturally and attract no attention until they could return to the café. Even then, they knew they had to be cautious. Circumstances might have changed since Nicholas had arranged the meeting, so as a precaution, they decided that Mike, being the linguist, would go in first to check that they were expected and that all was well, while Ronnie and Gris continued to walk about outside.

Time passed worryingly slowly until Mike reappeared to assure them that everything seemed in order, though he still needed to speak further with the two women to allay their remaining doubts. He then went back into the café, leaving Ronnie and Gris to keep circling the block – trying not to draw attention and longing for a chance to sit down and rest.

When Mike came out again, he had both good as well as somewhat disturbing news; they had been expected but were several hours early and the girls, unable to contact Nicholas, remained suspicious. The three were allowed in but if contact with Nicholas could not be made they would have to leave and walk about until he arrived; waiting inside indefinitely was not possible.

The café was small with a bar but only three tables; they chose the one furthest from the door and ordered a bottle of raspberry cordial. Mike whispered that the woman fetching their drink did not know who they were and it was her barmaid who was trying to talk to

Nicholas; it was a timely warning for as the woman brought their drink to the table she asked Mike in German who his friends were and what language they spoke. She did not seem convinced by his answer but asked no more questions and left them alone to drink their cordial. Mike had acquired some tobacco and rolled cigarettes for them that they duly smoked adding to the air of normality about their presence in the empty café. It was sometime before a man and a woman, both about 35 years old, came in together and after speaking to the owner and her barmaid, walked over to their table and said in German: 'Don't be afraid, we are friends of Nicholas and were expecting you this afternoon, you must come with us now to our flat'; as he spoke they noticed he had some gold teeth and duly referred to him, between themselves thereafter as 'Goldtooth'. The couple led them out into the street and onto a tram, paying the fares for a ten-minute ride to a large block of flats where they got off and were taken into a spacious apartment that the couple shared with Goldtooth's mother and two sisters, all of whom greeted them with delight. They accepted the offer of a bath without hesitation, the first real bath they had had for over a year, before enjoying an excellent meal and a short sleep. Their hosts woke them for supper after which conversation turned to their onward journey now that their plan of heading east to Russia had been ruled out. Staying in Warsaw was an option but getting back to England and joining the fight against Germany was their aim, no matter how safe and relatively comfortable they might be hiding in the city; there was also the consideration of what they might disclose if captured and interrogated under torture. Their conclusions before going to bed were to avoid anything that might endanger those helping them and, while listening to advice, to maintain their aim of getting back to England and the war against Germany.

Apart from waking up for a short time when air raid sirens went off, they slept soundly until woken to a breakfast of coffee and as much bread and jam as they could manage. Nicholas arrived while they were eating with the welcome news that all was now in place

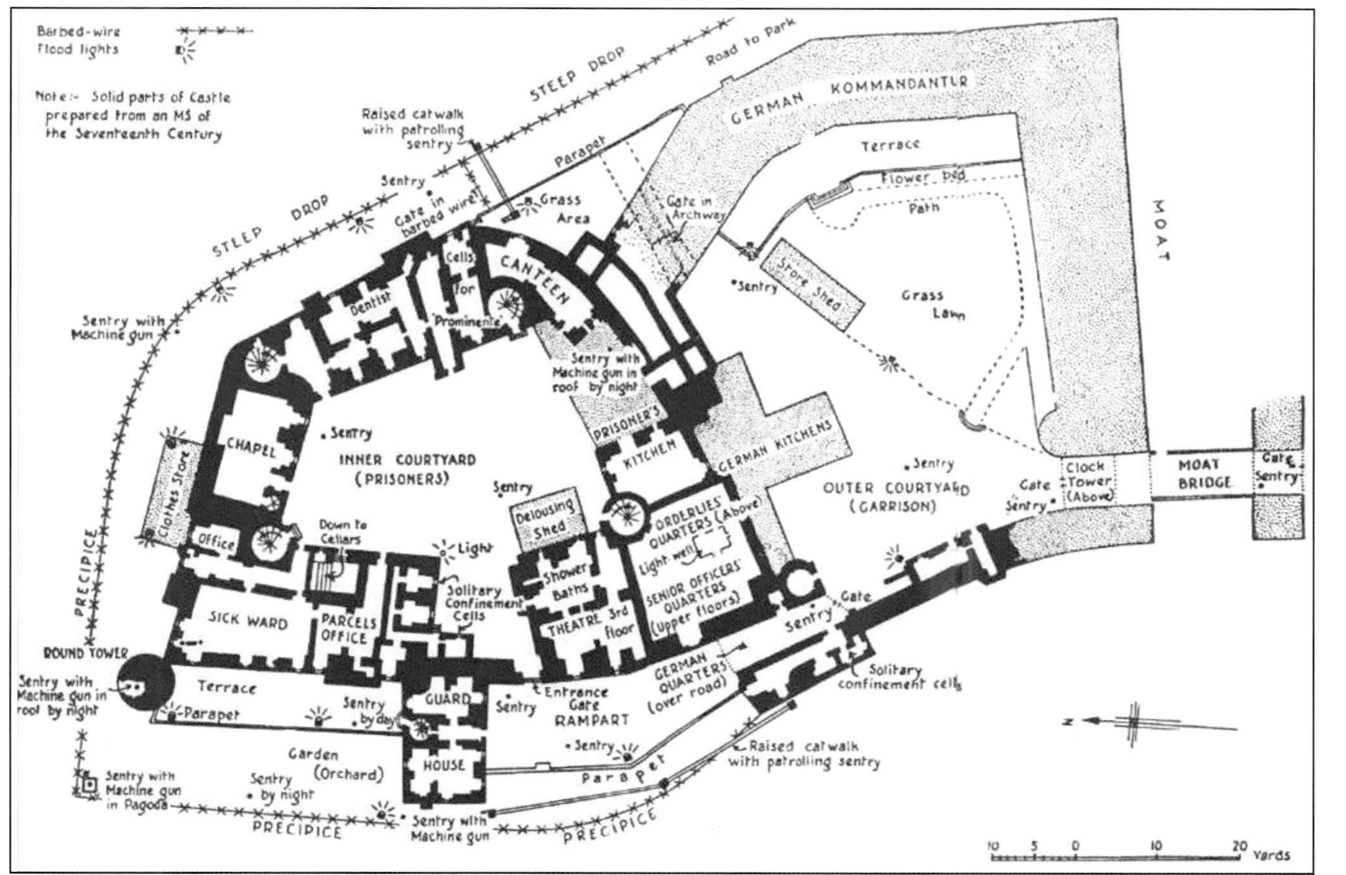

Diagram Colditz Castle with route of Feldwebel Rottenberg escape

Above left: Franz Josef

Above right: Jack Best

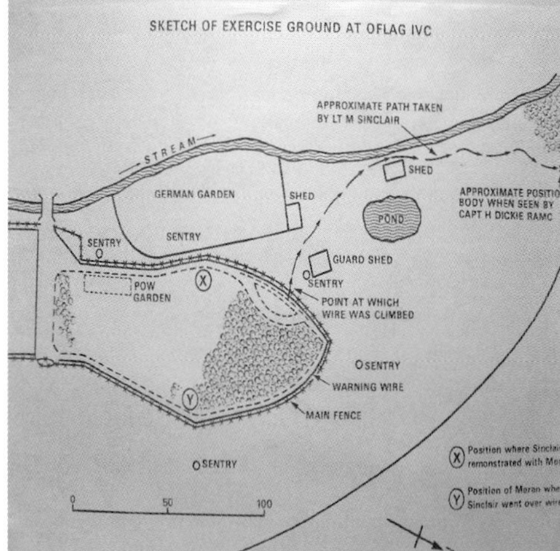

Above left: Final escape attempt from the Park

Above right: Mike Sinclair Grave Berlin Military Cemetery

and one of their names Sinclair" – who had been captured in Bulgaria. It was the last he was to hear of them until several months later, when he was greeted on arrival in Colditz by Mike himself.

The fear that the captured officers might be interrogated – or worse, tortured – and forced to reveal information prompted Gris to take his chance and attempt to reach Switzerland. Arrangements were made for him to set out in the second week of February, accompanied by Lance Corporal Weekes, another escapee being sheltered by the Poles. He spent his final day making a round of farewells to those who had sheltered and helped him, ending with a last cup of tea with Mrs M. Then, with Weekes beside him and Puffy as their guide, he made his way by tram to the railway station in Praga, the district of Warsaw on the east bank of the Vistula.

Accompanied by two Polish Secret Service agents, they travelled without incident to Kraków, arriving the following afternoon. There, they contacted the local Underground and were taken to a safe house. The door was opened by an enthusiastic man who greeted them in excellent English and assured them he could get them into Switzerland. He would provide new identity papers and travel passes for the journey, but for security reasons, he could say no more.

Later that evening, Puffy received a telephone call – a message from his wife warning him not to return home, as the Gestapo had learned of the escape organisation. He ignored the warning and was arrested upon his return.[4]

Gris and Lance Corporal Weekes remained in Krakow for several days before moving on, carrying the uneasy feeling that Mr X was too good to be true. The arrangements seemed thorough, however, and they were equipped with genuine documents issued by the 'White Russian Peoples Committee' in Berlin. They worked out histories of their lives, explaining why Gris spoke German but no Polish, and Weekes Polish but no German.

They refused the offer to carry arms, believing that if they were arrested it would compromise them as escaped POWs. After supper, they caught the Vienna Express, standing together in the corridor of the crowded train as it journeyed south to the Reich frontier. The train slowed and stopped at a station, where after a few minutes two policemen began checking papers – one inspecting people in the corridor, the other those in compartments. Gris had his documentation checked and returned with no comment. Weekes, however, did not understand what was being asked, and Gris had to intervene, explaining that Weekes only spoke German. This did not satisfy the policeman, and they had to accompany him into the station, avoiding the temptation to glance back at Mr X. They were subjected to a long question-and-answer session, during which they saw their train pull out to continue its journey to the frontier. It was a black moment. Their interrogators soon concluded that Gris spoke Polish quite fluently, but with a strong American or English accent, and decided a thorough investigation was needed. They were bundled into a car and delivered to a large police station back in Kracow.

Questioning began immediately and continued throughout the night. Gris, deciding that Mr X must by then have slipped away and alerted the escape organisation, felt it was time to confess their true identities as POWs from Posen. Since Posen had been closed for some time, this led to further questioning about who had assisted them while they were 'on the run' and whether they were in fact spies who would be shot. The interrogation went on until Gris took the initiative and stated firmly that he would give no information other than name, rank, and number, as required by the Geneva Convention. His interrogator paused, then ended his questions "for the moment." Gris was taken some distance to a civilian prison, where he was locked in a small cell containing a bed, basin, and lavatory, and given some food. He promptly went to sleep.

The next day passed uneventfully, but that night he was woken in the small hours and taken for further interrogation. He said nothing in response to the questions and was then presented with papers containing names, addresses, and details of the Warsaw Underground.

and they would be collected by 'a fat old lady' later in the morning who would take them to another safe location. When she arrived, accompanied by a younger woman, they were delighted to find that she spoke perfect English, albeit with a marked accent, and was in fact English by birth. She had settled in Warsaw after the end of the First World War, having married a Pole called Markowska and rather than struggle with the correct pronunciation they abbreviated her name between them to 'Mrs M'.[1] As a British subject she had been questioned by the Germans after their invasion of Poland and then released as 'an old lady of no importance' but contrary to their view she had soon established an underground operation to assist escaping POWs, mostly British, and had already helped many individuals to reach home via Russia, sadly a route now closed to them.[2]

After a fond farewell and heartfelt thanks to 'Goldtooth' and his wife, they took a tram with Mrs M and her companion to a building where they were taken to a back room that served as an office, and through it to a smaller room in which Mrs M lived with her husband, an older man whom she treated with ill-disguised disdain but affectionately called 'Daddy'. They learned that the room they were in was her headquarters looked after by 'Daddy', who lived there while she usually slept elsewhere. After a lunch prepared by "Daddy," they discussed their next steps. Hungary and the Balkan states had now entered the war, making them hostile territory. Mrs. M maintained that something could be arranged through her many contacts, though it would take time. While they waited, her Polish friends would shelter them, but they would have to move frequently to avoid attracting attention. She was already looking after half a dozen British soldiers "on the run," yet she seemed unconcerned about taking on one more. Not long after, a man arrived introducing himself as 'Mr Olszewski', not an easy name for them to pronounce and so, because of his prominent cheeks, he quickly became known to them as 'Puffy'.[3] He had been an international newspaper correspondent and was a good friend of Mrs M, forming with her the organisation that was now helping them; they came to like Puffy who was both charming and delightful company.

The three of them were split up to lessen the risk of detection and were provided with smarter clothing so they would blend into the population more readily. They were moved frequently, spending no more than five to six days in one place before being collected and taken elsewhere. Their hosts invariably seemed delighted to see and to help them despite the risks they ran in giving them shelter; the majority spoke either English, French or German, which was a relief as none of the three escapees could converse in Polish. They ventured out very occasionally with their hosts to a café or restaurant but mostly stayed indoors reading, playing patience and trying to improve their spoken German. On the whole, life seemed remarkably normal in the city apart from the number of uniformed Germans on the streets, soldiers, airmen, police and SS[4]; none of whom interfered in Polish life unless they perceived something was against German interests. Civil policing was the role of seemingly Polish police, but many were '*Volksdeutsche*', ethnic Germans, and not to be trusted; the few Poles in the police force passed on information to the Underground about police intentions and planned operations that enabled Mrs M to stay one step ahead of them. The Polish Underground did carry out occasional acts of sabotage, inevitably sparking mass arrests by the Germans and the interrogation, under torture, of anyone believed to have been involved. Some suspects were shot out of hand; others were sent to concentration camps – places about which little was known at the time – where relatives received no news unless the individual had died or been killed. In such cases, bizarrely, the family would receive a parcel containing the person's shoes, but no other personal effects or information.

At other times, mass arrests took place when police and soldiers suddenly surrounded an area for no apparent reason other than to terrorise the population. Those carrying papers that showed they were working for the Germans were left alone; others were seized without compassion and sent away to be put to work, somewhere and in some capacity unknown. Mothers were forcibly separated from their children, and fathers were beaten if they tried to intervene. There was no law to protect the Polish population from the whims of their conquerors.

Shops and restaurants were surprisingly well stocked, and the food situation was generally satisfactory. For those with cash, eggs, meat, vegetables, and fruit – as well as bread and sugar – were plentiful. But for those without ready money, it was a hungry time. The official ration allowance, which could be purchased, provided just enough to stave off starvation but no more. The reason given was that *"Poles required less to eat than Germans."*

For those living in the ghetto, conditions were far worse. Surrounded by a high wall, it was overcrowded and equipped with only the most rudimentary sanitary arrangements – completely inadequate for the numbers confined there, despite many having already been deported to concentration camps or murdered by the SS. All movement in or out was strictly controlled, and boarding or leaving the trams that passed through the ghetto was forbidden. Inside the walls, as they had observed in Lodz, every man, woman, and child wore a yellow Star of David – a requirement enforced by the German-appointed Jewish police who patrolled the area.

News of the war was broadcast over loudspeakers on the streets and reported in both Polish and German-language newspapers. These "official" sources, however, were not regarded as trustworthy by most Poles, who instead relied on BBC broadcasts, listened to in secret on hidden radios and passed on by word of mouth.

Shortly after their arrival, Mrs M took Mike and Gris to a friend's flat to hear one of these broadcasts from London. Gris later recalled: *"I shall never forget my excitement at hearing again, after so long, the chimes of Big Ben. They sent out, somehow, a message of encouragement and hope, and proof that 'home' really did exist."*

The morale of the Poles, whether rich or poor, was high, collectively they gave the impression that collaboration with the

Germans was unthinkable no matter how much they suffered as a result; non-cooperation was a matter of national pride and nothing it seemed would alter the deeply rooted belief that their future lay in friendship with the West and not in closer relations with the Russians. For the escapees, life at that time was both comfortable and secure, yet the need to live separately – and to spend most of their time indoors, reading or reflecting on their situation – made it a lonely and monotonous existence.

Gradually, as they began to feel more at ease, and more conscious of the danger they posed to those sheltering them, they realised that leading a more normal life would draw less attention to themselves – and, in turn, to their hosts. With this in mind, they began to venture out alone and mingle with people on the streets. For Mike, who was entirely at ease speaking German, and for Gris – whose command of the language was by now almost fluent – this posed no difficulty. If asked a casual question, both could reply with confidence. Ronnie, however, had not acquired the same fluency and therefore did not go out unless accompanied by one of the others.

Meanwhile, Mrs M and Puffy were hard at work, slowly piecing together a plan to get the three men safely on their way. Although they had useful contacts, they had been unable to make progress on any of the options they considered. Eventually, they narrowed the possibilities to three for detailed consideration: Sweden, via a Baltic port – as Peter Douglas had done, though they were unaware at the time of his "home run" success; Turkey, via the Balkans, Switzerland, and Yugoslavia, with help from the guerrillas there; or Russia, despite the ongoing German blitzkrieg. (Annex B)

Each option had its drawbacks, but all shared one serious obstacle: the difficulty of obtaining the necessary personal documents. Most importantly, there was the danger their continued presence posed to those sheltering and helping them. If they were caught, the three would likely be sent back to a prison camp, but anyone found to have assisted them would almost certainly be interrogated and either shot

Gris realized that, since the organisation had been compromised, he was unlikely to be put under pressure to disclose anything more. On being returned to his cell, he discovered that Weekes was in a nearby cell. It proved impossible to communicate with him, and with nothing to do, boredom soon set in – displaced only by a raging toothache, alleviated by a friendly guard who brought him five codeine tablets he had bought with his own money, along with a cigarette – but regrettably no matches. Gris tried to light the cigarette from the stove without success and suffered torment until he finally got a match.

After two days he was informed by one of the guards that a General was due to visit and that he was not to speak, even if addressed by him; his immediate reaction was to rehearse in his mind what he would say if the General did come to the cell. His opportunity came the next day and, ignoring the guards, he stepped forward and spoke: 'Herr General I am a British officer POW who has escaped and been recaptured. I have a comrade, a Corporal also in this prison. I request we be returned to the custody of the German army.'

There was no response from the General who, after a few seconds gazing at Gris, turned and walked out leaving him once more locked in his cell alone. Three days passed and then he was told that he and Corporal Weekes were to leave the next day. The following morning after a wash and shave their belongings were returned and escorted by several German soldiers, they marched to the station. After travelling all day, they reached a large camp for British ORs at Lamsdorf. In a brief conversation that they managed on the journey Weekes was able to assure Gris that he had said nothing that might be useful to the Germans; they were parted on arrival at Lamsdorf, Weekes entering the POW camp and Gris spending a night in the cell block, before being collected by a *Feldwebel* and several soldiers for his onward journey to Oflag IV-C.

CHAPTER 8

ON THE RUN

Not long after Gris' departure, Mike, Ronnie and the three Poles were also on their way. Following five days and six nights of cross-country travel, however, they needed to smarten their appearances if they were not to be too conspicuous in public. Mike and Ronnie had a shaving kit as well as boot cleaning brushes and polish to help maintain a respectable appearance; the Poles were carrying a change of clothing. Their train arrived in Budapest around four in the afternoon of 31 May where the arrangements that had been made to help them worked smoothly again and they were met to be taken to a safe house. They were in the house for only a few days before being moved to a pension where they stayed for a month, taking all their meals in the room they shared together and venturing out infrequently, while arrangements were being made for their onward journey. In case they were caught up in one of the frequent spot-checks on the streets, they had been provided with passes by the Polish underground which showed them to be Polish internees on leave in Budapest from a Hungarian internment camp; however, it was not long before the local Police began to make enquiries about these passes. As a precaution they were moved, given new documentation made out in different names and then separated for a short time as a further safeguard. The following months passed uneventfully, and it was not until the second week of November that they were contacted to be sent by train with six others into Yugoslavia, carrying papers that showed them to be Volksdeutsche – people whose language and culture had German origins but who did not hold German citizenship. They travelled to Szeged, arriving around 10 am, from where they walked across the frontier and boarded a train to Pancevo about ten miles south of Belgrade, arriving there at 1 pm in the afternoon of 10 November and queuing with many others for the ferry to cross the Danube – the boarding of which was carefully controlled by German troops. Passes and luggage were being inspected by a uniformed German official, but in the crush, Ronnie was waved through unchecked while Mike and the others were required to show their documents, which they did without incident. The crossing took three quarters of an hour and on landing there was another slightly less careful check of documentation before they were cleared and allowed on their way. Taken to a safe house by one of the group, they were given a meal before settling down for a welcome sleep.

Waking the following day they caught a train to Jagodina, some seventy miles south, where their guides left them in a safe house and returned to Budapest. The town was garrisoned by around 200 German soldiers from different arms and services, said to have come from the Russian front; they did not appear to be very active and the escapees felt quite secure there. After five days, on 16 November, Ronnie and Mike set off by train for Sofia with two Polish women, one of whom left them en route at a small town four hours into their journey, while the other, a heavily pregnant 22-year-old woman who could speak Serbian and was hoping to be able to join her husband in Turkey, stayed with them. At 6 am, they left in a horse-drawn cart for a journey of about twenty-five miles along side roads, aiming to cross the frontier into Pirot in Bulgaria. They passed a number of Yugoslav border posts who took no notice of them and shortly after pulled into a Serb-owned farm that straddled the line of the frontier; the farmer led them around a border post to a village on the Bulgarian side where it had been arranged they would be met and taken on by cart to Pirot and beyond. It was now that the arrangements began to go wrong; the owner of the cart was not at home and the farmer guiding them quickly asked a friend of his to find another. While following this man along a country road they had the misfortune to meet a Bulgarian Customs Official and aroused his curiosity. He asked for their passes and demanded to check their baggage; on examining their documents and realising they had Yugoslavian and not Bulgarian passes they were ordered to follow him. The Polish girl advised them it would be wiser to obey him, and that they should be able to bluff him without too much difficulty. They were then escorted back to Pirot by Customs officials and questioned by the Commander of the local Customs Guards. Mike and the Polish girl, speaking in German, told him that they were German but their bluff was called when he immediately offered to contact Germans nearby who might be able to help them. This was not an offer they had anticipated, or welcomed, and quickly changed their story claiming they were really Poles. The reaction to this news was sympathetic from all bar one of the officials, but nevertheless all three of them were taken to the Police Headquarters in Pirot and handed over to Bulgarian police who questioned Mike and the girl, but not Ronnie, before taking them to the gaol and locking them in separate cells for the next two days, where they were treated quite reasonably.

Early on 19 November they were moved by train under police escort to Sofia, arriving there at 8 am. They were given breakfast before being taken to the CID where they were fingerprinted and asked to write out statements in French with the help of a female Bulgarian interpreter. Once this was done they were taken to a local jail where Mike and Ronnie were put into a small, filthy, vermin-infested cell with six others, all Bulgarian men, on a bread and water diet; they found out later that their female companion was held in similarly poor conditions in the woman's part of the prison. A day later all three, Mike, Ronnie and the girl, were moved to separate and cleaner cells in the Police Headquarters prison and left undisturbed for several days before being questioned separately. Mike and Ronnie managed to converse briefly and agreed on the story that Mike was a Polish student attempting to leave Poland and that Ronnie was a Pole living in America who had been visiting relations in Poland before travelling to Hungary just before the outbreak of war. Their interrogator told them, separately, that their stories were false and all three of them, the girl included, would be handed over to German authorities unless they told the truth. On hearing this Mike chose to reveal that he was in fact a British Officer POW on the run, to which his interrogator promptly replied that if he gave the full details of the route he had taken, and those who had helped him, he would be sent to Turkey with Ronnie and the girl. Ronnie was the next to be questioned by which time his interrogator knew from what Mike had revealed that he was an officer and escaped POW; he was told, as Mike had been, that if he gave a detailed account of his route and anyone who had assisted him, he would be sent to Turkey within a few days. Ronnie was suspicious and so, as he and Mike had previously discussed, began to write a statement in English listing imaginary routes and helpers. As he was writing Mike was brought in and spoke to him in French 'Nous devons dire la vérité' – we must tell the truth – and was then quickly taken out again leaving Ronnie puzzled and wondering if Mike had been tortured or had some unpleasant experience under interrogation that he had not. After some thought he decided that he would follow Mike's advice and duly wrote out a true statement of their routes and helpers.

Returned to their separate cells they did not see one another until five days later when they met unexpectedly in the prison barbers' shop on 27 November. Mike managed to signal to Ronnie that things had gone wrong before they were separated and returned to their cells. A short while later they met again while being taken to collect their belongings and managed a short conversation; Mike said he had been told by the Chief of Police that it was no longer possible to send them to Turkey, citing that Bulgaria had now signed the Anti-Comintern Pact, an agreement between Germany, Italy and Japan, to work together to stop the spread of Communism that was aimed at Russia, and that the Germans already knew of their whereabouts; this was a worry that they could not talk about in detail because of the presence in the room of a German NCO, who they believed understood English. Mike had refused to say anything while this NCO was present and had demanded to speak to the police official who had seen them initially, a request that was eventually granted. Mike then protested vigorously that their statements had been made solely because they had received assurances that the documents would not be passed to the Germans. Eventually he was given the statements and permitted to burn them; when he asked if any copies had been made, he was assured none had. A short time later they had an opportunity for a brief conversation with the Polish girl who told them that subsequent to the burning of the original statements she had noticed a typed copy of one of them on the desk of the interrogator who had seen them initially, but before they could do anything about it all three of them were taken under escort to the jail in Sofia and then, late on 27 May, put in a special wing that was under German control. En route to the jail Ronnie managed to ask an English-speaking Bulgarian police official to inform the American Consul of their situation but his request was ignored.

A few days later, on 30 November, Ronnie was taken before two plain-clothes Bulgarian police and told he could write a letter to his father but must not say where he was. He protested strongly about the way he and Mike were being treated by the Bulgarians and demanded to see the Chief of Police as he was particularly anxious to prevent the Polish girl being handed over to the Germans. He was immediately asked if she was an agent and was able to reassure them that all she had done was to use her knowledge of Balkan dialects to help him and Mike reach Bulgaria. Two days later Ronnie, Mike and the girl were taken by train under escort to Belgrade, where the girl was handed over to a German soldier while they were taken 150 miles by train to the military prison in Vienna. They remained there over

Christmas and the New Year and were well treated; there is no record of what happened to the girl.

On the morning of 17 January, Mike and Ronnie were taken to the city's Franz Joseph train station escorted by an Austrian *feldwebel* and a private, who both sat in the same compartment with them. This was the start of Mike's journey to Colditz, where his most audacious escape attempt centred on his impersonation of *Feldwebel* Rottenberger, who bore a striking resemblance to the late Emperor Franz Joseph of Austria, an interesting coincidence! At one point, when the private left their compartment to stretch his legs for a few minutes, the *feldwebel* spoke candidly to them expressing his dislike for Germans, and in particular the way in which they ill-treated Russian POWs; he also revealed that his orders were to take them to a place near Dresden, but did not reveal the name of it. When an opportunity came Mike and Ronnie managed to have a short talk and agreed that they should attempt to escape from the train rather than run the risk of being handed over to the German authorities at the end of their journey.

They recced a lavatory and, without being detected, managed to break the supports that held the window in place before returning to their compartment to await a chance to jump off the train. It would be a risky attempt; even if they were successful, they had no money and no food, except the meagre amount they had saved from their lunch earlier in the day; on the plus side, they were still in respectable plain clothes with soft hats in their pockets, and had their washing and shaving kits. Between Prague and Roudnice, still some distance from Dresden, and for no apparent reason, the train began to slow down, making jumping off without serious injury suddenly seem feasible. It was the opportunity they had been waiting for and, on the pretext of needing to relieve himself, Mike left the compartment escorted by the *feldwebel* who remained in the corridor while Mike went into the lavatory. Ronnie followed a few minutes later having asked the private for permission to stand in the corridor beside the *feldwebel* 'to get some air'. They had arranged that if Mike found he was able to get out of the lavatory window he would leave the door latch in a certain position and as Ronnie got into the corridor, seeing the latch was in the position they had agreed, he walked past the *feldwebel* and went into the lavatory, locking the door behind him. He quickly climbed out through the window feet first and hung onto the side of the train, realising it was now picking up speed again. He felt a touch on his leg and looking down saw Mike below him on the step of the train so climbed down to join him. Together they made their way to the buffers between two coaches and were standing there as the train slowed down once more approaching Roudnice station. Seeing his opportunity Mike jumped off, landing clear of the train but awkwardly, twisting his ankle and slightly dazing himself in the process; at that same moment a door in the carriage opened and the *feldwebel* looked out, he spotted Mike but failed to see Ronnie, who was still on the buffers and crouching just out of sight. The train stopped almost immediately and the *feldwebel* and a private jumped off to pursue Mike, catching him quickly as he tried to limp away on his sprained ankle. Believing that Ronnie must have jumped off the train as well, the *feldwebel* and the private then began to search the area and were joined by two railway police who stood on the side of the track just below where Ronnie was hiding, flashing their torches about as they discussed Mike's escape attempt. As they moved along, carefully searching the immediate area with the aid of their torches, a timely escape of steam obscured Ronnie from their view and he remained undiscovered. It was the second occasion during an escape attempt, the discovery of the tunnel in Laufen being the first, on which Mike was caught while Ronnie avoided discovery.

With Mike captured, the hue and cry immediately around the train and in the surrounding area died down, allowing Ronnie to slip off the buffers and walk quickly southwards along the railway line. It was bitterly cold and without an overcoat he realised he needed to find a helper quickly if he was to avoid hypothermia. After a few minutes weighing his options, he decided his best course of action in the circumstances was to walk back about three miles to Roudnice and try his luck finding a sympathetic and friendly householder. Knowing he was in Czechoslovakia he decided to speak in German when speaking to anyone who appeared to be a potential helper; if they replied in bad German or Czech, he would tell them who he was, but if their response was in fluent German, he would move on as soon as he could without arousing suspicion and approach someone else. His plan worked well and on his third attempt a boy of about 17 years old befriended him and took him home, telling him to wait while he fetched a relative who had lived in America and spoke English. The boy was true to his word, Ronnie was duly collected and taken to his home by the boy's relative, where he stayed for the next two nights and, very generously, was given a big jacket to wear in lieu of an overcoat, a pair of boots and a small sum of money. He had hoped to get contact details of someone in Prague who might help him, but his helpers knew no one; he was directed to an address in Krabcice, 23 miles north of Prague, where there was a person who could assist him. Although it was probably safe, he was advised to walk rather than risk a train journey, and to ask for a lift on a coal lorry if one came by; however, that seemed an unnecessary risk to take and he duly decided to set off on foot to cover the 40-odd miles to Prague using side roads; he stopped to buy a hot drink at an Inn and shortly after, having covered 25 miles and feeling exhausted as much by the cold as anything else, decided to chance his luck and seek help. After a short period of hesitancy, he approached someone and after explaining that he was a POW 'on the run', was directed to a farm where he met two workers. They were curious and inquisitive about his identity, but he felt safe in telling them the truth; to his horror, one of them replied 'I am a German!' Fortunately, he appeared none too bright and seemed content merely to tell Ronnie to go away which, relieved, he did immediately and headed off towards Prague, catching a train that arrived in the city centre at 7 pm. He had been given an address but there was no reply to his knocking and it was clear that the individual he had hoped to meet was away; very tired and lame he tried without success to find somewhere to shelter from the bitter cold and returned to the railway station to sit out the night. Around 1 am, dozing intermittently despite the cold, he noticed the police moving around checking passes and went back out onto the street to avoid them. Deciding to take a chance he approached a man who, to his relief, listened to his story and took him to an all-night restaurant where he was able to wait safely in the warm until morning.

Early on 25 January Ronnie returned to the address he had been given, this time with success meeting the individual he had hoped to see who asked him for an example of his handwriting and told him to return that afternoon once his identity had been thoroughly checked. Once accepted as genuine, he explained that his plan was to try to reach Switzerland once the snow had melted and the passes through the mountains were clear, which he estimated would be in about two months; his contact agreed to help him. He was taken to a flat in the city and remained in hiding over the next four months, moving several times to maintain security. On 18 May, a helper took him by train the 87 miles to Husinec. Two days later another helper accompanied him on the 180-mile train journey to Linz and a safe house. He stayed there overnight before travelling on alone to Innsbruck, taking slow trains and buying third-class tickets in stages, hoping to avoid arousing any interest; in Salzburg he needed to change trains and managed to do so without arousing any interest or prompting any questions. He finally arrived in Innsbruck at eight in the morning of 22 May and went straight to the address he had been given – only to find his contact, and potential helper, ill in bed and unable to help or advise him; he decided to travel on nevertheless. At 2 pm, having taken a slow train, he arrived in Bludenz some 90 miles away, a town nestling in a valley at the foot of the Alps – close, he assumed, to the Swiss border where thick snow still lay. Walking around the town he spotted an elderly man working in his garden and decided to tell his story and seek advice on the feasibility of crossing the mountains into Switzerland. The reply he got was disappointing; the snow was impassable, and the frontier strongly guarded. Somewhat downhearted Ronnie went to the nearby Lion Hotel for a drink before finding a barn and bedding down for the night.

Waking early on 23 May he returned to the railway station and caught a train to Schruns, sixteen miles further south down the valley, where he was fortunate to find a retired priest who spoke English and in answer to his query confirmed that it would be impossible to cross the mountains into Switzerland until later in the year when the snow had melted; his opinion was shared by another local Ronnie approached a little later. Believing that nearby Lichenstein was occupied, he decided to cut his losses and return to Husinec and make another attempt in June when the snow had melted; it took him two days to complete the return journey via Linz and Prachatice, where he had to rest for two days due to a high temperature. He was up and regaining strength on 27 May when in the evening the news reached him through his helper that Reinhard Heydrich, acting governor of the Protectorate of Bohemia and Moravia and a principal architect of the Holocaust, had been ambushed and wounded in Prague that day by a team of Czech and Slovak soldiers, trained by the British SOE, who had been sent by the Czechoslovak government-in-exile to kill him; police activities in search of those involved were widespread.[1] Ronnie's situation was precarious, as it was for those continuing to help him, and he decided his best option was to make his way to Prague where it would be easier to remain hidden in the large population. Two days later, on 29 May, his luck deserted him when a Czech Gendarme asked for his pass as he tried to board a train in Husinec. Hoping to be able to bluff his way out of danger Ronnie spoke to him in German, telling him that he had lost his pass, but was arrested nevertheless; knowing that the Gendarme was a Czech, and not a Sudetenlander sympathetic to the Germans, Ronnie revealed his true identity and asked for help. The reply was short, 'On no account', and the Gendarme kept a very close eye on him thereafter to ensure he did not give him the slip.

A few hours later Ronnie was taken thirty miles east to Budweis and handed over to the German Criminal Police, where he was photographed and fingerprinted before being questioned about his escape and shown a list of missing persons that contained his name; he told his interrogators the POW camps he had been in, but invented the names of his helpers and the routes he had taken. The next day, 30 May, he was handcuffed and taken to the Gestapo Headquarters in Prague where he was interrogated for seven hours a day for three days, but well treated initially with a break for lunch, brought to him from the canteen, and accommodated at night in a building outside the Gestapo offices. After three days he was put into solitary confinement where he remained for six weeks, being called out for questioning only twice. He was kept on a starvation diet and given drinking water only at meal times - if thirsty between meals his only option was to drink from the lavatory bowl in his cell. On 15 July he was moved to a military prison in Prague and two days later, escorted by a *feldwebel* and a soldier, he was taken by train to Oflag-IV C, Colditz Castle. On the journey, perhaps learning from experience, his escort did not allow him to use the lavatory.

On his arrival at Colditz, Ronnie was soon looking, once again, for opportunities to escape and it was only three months later that the Escape Committee approved an idea he put forward with Lieutenant Commander William Stephens, RNVR, to break out through the German *Kommandantur* kitchen along with a second pair of prisoners, one of whom should have some lock-picking ability, and gain access to the roof from where they would be able to escape into the surrounding countryside. The plan was approved and Captain Pat Reid[2] and Flight Lieutenant Howard Wardle were selected to join them; the plan was put into practice on 14 October. The four-man group gained access to the German kitchen, crossed the yard into, and then out of, the Kommandantur cellar to access the dry moat.

From there, with several near discoveries on the way by patrolling sentries, they used a sheet to descend three terraces and reach the road that led away through the woods; it was by then the early morning of 15 October, as they separated into their two groups and set off for Switzerland. Pat Reid and Howard Wardle reached and crossed the Swiss border three days later on 18 October, followed at 3 am in the morning of 20 October by Ronnie and William Stephens. Ronnie left Switzerland on 25 January 1943, and with Flight Lieutenant Hedley Fowler, who had escaped earlier from Colditz, travelled across unoccupied France crossing into Spain on 30 January 1943, only to be arrested by the Spanish authorities later the same day. They were taken to a military prison at Figueras, where they were held in filthy and cramped conditions until 22 February, when they were taken to the British Consul in Barcelona. From there they travelled to Gibraltar, arriving on 25 March 1943 and from there onto England.

Ronnie returned to active duty in June 1944 as Second-in-Command of 2 KRRC assuming command of the battalion in Normandy at the end of July from Lieutenant Colonel Heathcote-Amory. The battalion was ordered forward on 1 September to occupy and hold a village eight miles from their night leaguer; he went ahead in his scout car to recce the objective in advance of the main body, who were slow getting started. As he neared the village a German anti-tank gun fired on his vehicle at point-blank range, killing him, his driver and the gunner Battery Commander who was with him instantly.

CHAPTER 9

OFLAG IV-C COLDITZ

The small town of Colditz lay thirty miles southeast of Leipzig in the heart of Hitler's Reich, and some 400 miles from any frontier not under Nazi control; there, on a steep, rocky hill overlooking the Mulde River that flowed through the town, sat Colditz Castle. A former residence of the Kings of Saxony, the castle had served many purposes since then as prison, sanatorium for the wealthy, lunatic asylum and hospital; when the Nazis gained power during 1933, they converted the castle into a political prison for communists, homosexuals, Jews and other people they considered undesirable. It was first used as a prisoner-of-war camp in 1939 for Polish officers who were replaced after the fall of France in 1940 by Belgian officers, most of whom were released on general parole later that year. Subsequently empty it became: '*Oflag IV-C, lager mit besonderer Bewachung.*' – 'A special Officers' camp with strict surveillance of prisoners.'

It was, in effect, a maximum-security prison for escape-prone Allied Officers under Article 48 of the Geneva Convention. The outer walls of the castle dominating the small town below were 7ft thick at their base, and the cliff on which it was built had a sheer drop of 250ft to the north-flowing river below, making it impregnable for any assailant; but it had been designed to keep people out rather than in, and the only modification made for the latter purpose had been putting bars on the windows. The original walls were now topped with barbed wire and overlooked by sentry boxes perched at intervals around the buildings that were swept by searchlights from dusk to dawn. Staffed by numerous armed guards and located a very long way from friendly territory, Colditz Castle seemed to offer no hope of escape for any prisoners held there.[1] As Phil Pardoe wrote when he arrived at Colditz: 'The first impression was not encouraging – a gigantic *schloss* with barred windows. Standing upright on a sheer hillock and surrounded by many miles of wire and sentry boxes perched on top of tall poles it looked depressing to live in and hard to escape from.'

They caught an afternoon train and were approaching their destination as dusk fell on a cold winter evening, it was mid-March 1942. When the train slowed the *Feldwebel* turned to Gris; 'Look out of the window Herr Lieutenant, now you can see Colditz Castle, beautiful is it not?' Gris looked and got his first glimpse of Colditz.

Walking up from the station early that winter evening the closer Gris got to the castle the more formidable it seemed; it was only a short walk with his escort but nevertheless a tiring uphill tramp carrying his belongings along the cobbled streets to the outer gate of the castle. The gate was unlocked and Gris was taken across the courtyard of the German area of the castle to an office, where his particulars were noted down by the Duty Officer before he was locked in a cell beneath the main archway for the rest of the night. Early the next morning he was escorted into the prisoners' area of the castle, at that time of the day an empty courtyard surrounded by high walls with many barred windows. As was the set procedure for any new arrival, Gris was 'deloused' by taking a very hot, and very welcome, shower while his clothing was heat-treated to kill any eggs lurking in the seams; to his relief he did not have to suffer the indignity of having his head shaved as had happened in Laufen: 'This was the first decent wash I had had since leaving Warsaw. Even the soap and clean towel which were provided seemed luxury indeed!'

As he finished showering and was drying himself, to his delight Mike appeared in the shower block carrying a slice of bread, lavishly spread with margarine and jam, which he offered to Gris. Taken aback by this unexpected generosity Gris at first refused to accept what he presumed had been put together from Mike's rations. However, reassured by Mike's explanation that contrary to his experiences as a POW to date, things were different in Colditz where Red Cross parcels were plentiful and received regularly, and so Gris gratefully consumed 'the best bit of food since my recapture', before being released into the prisoners' yard and accommodation.

The claustrophobic nature of the castle quickly became apparent to Gris, as it did for all new arrivals. The irregular shaped courtyard was small, about 37 x 24 yards in size, and was the main exercise area for the prisoners; in the mornings it would be occupied by numerous individuals doing their daily routine of stretches and exercises; later in the day, weather permitting, it was occupied by the sun worshippers who were constantly moving to follow any patches of sunlight that managed to reach the cobblestones despite the shadows cast by the high surrounding buildings. Usually quite busy throughout the day the courtyard would be vacated periodically for games of 'stoolball', a typically eccentric English Public School type of game, that derived its name from the stool occupied by each team's goalkeeper. Opposing teams were supposed to keep running with the ball, bouncing it occasionally, the aim being to score a goal by touching it on the other sides' stool. Although major injuries were few, the matches were quite violent; those who possessed the ball could, and would, do anything to keep it. As a result, crashing into each other, pulling hair and tearing clothes were common occurrences, all accompanied by loud shouts and the cheering of supporters, but unwritten fair-play rules were followed and tripping was out of question. When a match was on the courtyard would be left free for the 'stoolballers', while spectators would watch from their room windows.

The 1929 Geneva Convention stated that: 'prisoners shall have facilities for engaging in physical exercises and obtaining the benefit of being out of doors',[2] but many prisoners took their daily exercise by walking around the courtyard in preference to going through the formalities and checks required before being allowed into the barbed-wire surrounded field below the castle, somewhat disparagingly known as 'the park', the nearest open area that met the specified requirement in the Convention of being 'outside and ideal for taking exercise'. Those wishing to enjoy the illusion of freedom it gave and were prepared to accept the protracted checks required by the German guards before setting off, were 'marched down' to enjoy the grass underfoot and bird song in the trees that provided a welcome respite from the cobbles and austere nature of the courtyard.

'Marched down' does not, however, describe a simple process of moving prisoners to the park; the POWs had to be escorted, and so to justify the number of the castle guard force needed to guarantee security, there had to be at least thirty prisoners to be marched down. The prisoners formed up in five ranks between the guardroom and the approach yard to be counted, not the straightforward task it might seem with individuals darting back through the gate to call for a person to join them before setting off, escorted by several guards under command of a SNCO or officer. It was never a very orderly procession; individuals walked along at varied speeds, chatting and inevitably out of step, around the north of the castle and down the steep path to the enclosed area, where they halted while the guards made a second count before dispersing to positions round the outside of the enclosure. Crossing the low warning wire running two yards from the perimeter fence and marking the limit of the permitted exercise area was forbidden; even approaching it ran the risk of being shot. The prisoners would sometimes play 'football' in the park, with rules allowing them to hide behind the trees and jump out suddenly if and when there was an opportunity to score a goal; it was a much better game than regular football as far as the prisoners were concerned.

The park also offered a prime opportunity for escape, with an early and successful example being Pierre Mairesse-Lebrun – a Captain in the Chasseurs de l'Afrique captured in 1940 and sent to Colditz. On 1 July 1941 he and Lieutenant Pierre Odry were doing gymnastics in the park and when the guards were distracted while assembling the POWs to return to the castle, they took their chance and ran to the fence. Odry, with his back to the wire, catapulted Lebrun over the fence who then ran off into the woods; the guards started shooting after their initial surprise, but he got away unscathed. Still in his sports clothes, Lebrun hid in a field until the initial search for him was called off and then made his way over several days to Vichy France via Switzerland, making himself out to be an individual jogging along the roads taking exercise by day and sleeping rough at night. He left a note in his room:

> 'Should I succeed I would be obliged for the dispatch of my effects to me at: Lieut Pierre Marisse-Lebrun, Orange (Vackluse). May God help me.'

The Germans obliged!

CHAPTER 10

THE ESCAPING GAME

In *Kriegsgefangen offiziers sonderlager 4C* (Colditz), the German guard force was led by Hauptman Rheinhold Eggers, a veteran of the First World War in which he had fought on the Western Front, winning three awards for bravery. He and those he commanded were in a continual battle of wits with the resourceful prisoners, but he always treated them correctly and ensured that his subordinates did so as well. Lieutenant Damiaen J. van Doorninck, a Dutch POW in Colditz, wrote of him: 'This man was our opponent, but nevertheless he earned our respect by his correct attitude, self-control and total lack of rancour despite all the harassment we gave him.'

Valuable items 'acquired' by various means, or made by prisoners, were concealed from the German guard force in 'hides' that became increasingly sophisticated as the officers explored their area of the castle and found rooms and spaces of which the Germans were unaware. Escaping was akin to a game as well as their duty for the prisoners in Colditz; Hauptman Eggers kept a record of the four years he spent as one of the '*Lager Offizier*' in the camp guard force, that shows over 300 prisoners were caught in the act of escaping. The figure is a little misleading as in several instances it was the same individuals trying time and again; Eggers further noted that 'on 130 occasions escapers got out of the castle or got away in transit locally'. Most were quickly recaptured and only thirty got clean away from Colditz, six Dutch, fourteen French, nine British and one Pole;

however, another eight Colditz prisoners escaped and made home runs while in the custody of others, responsibility having been signed over to them; of the eight, seven escaped while in transit to or from hospital appointments, and one from prison while awaiting court martial.

One method of concealing highly prized and sometimes irreplaceable documents from the Germans was to use what were referred to colloquially as 'arse creepers'; the name originated from the cigars sent to Pat Reid that arrived in containers labelled 'H Upmann, Havana', and were ideal for holding small items like maps, button compasses, money and stolen or forged passes. After being smeared with Vaseline they were inserted into the rectum, not always an easy or comfortable thing to do as Airey Neave found when preparing for his escape attempt in August 1941:

> I was handed a mysterious cigar-shaped container about two and a half inches long … in which to conceal the (German) money that had come from black market deals with the guards. It was explained to me that to avoid its capture if I did not get out of the camp, I must carry it ... inside my rectum and if not found (in any German searches) return it.[1]

When being used, arse creepers had to be retrieved after a bowel movement and reinserted, not a pleasant business; it was said that the French were fastidious and for reasons of hygiene used to attach a thread to their arse creepers so they could be removed prior to settling down in the latrines. The story, whether true or not, went around the British that an especially diligent German conducting a body search of some French prisoners had noticed threads protruding from their anuses; curious about what he was seeing he elected to pull them with disastrous consequences for the French escaping effort! On another occasion a prisoner managed to escape but was quickly recaptured and returned to Colditz. There was an immediate sentence of thirty days in 'solitary' for attempting to escape, but before he was locked up his messmates were able to give him a hot meal of Red X stew and cocoa; then, comfortably full, he was taken away to start his sentence. En route he was permitted to stop off at the latrines from where after a short interval came the sound of a lavatory flushing followed immediately by an anguished cry; he had failed to remove his arse creeper and washed away all of his carefully gathered Reich Marks.

'Goon baiting' was a pastime enjoyed and practised by all prisoners at every opportunity. On one occasion during an '*Appel*', the Germans asked for volunteers from among the assembled POWs to work for them outside the prison. Quite unexpectedly, and to the surprise and disdain of all on parade, a French prisoner stepped forward as a volunteer and announced that he would like to work for the Germans. There was a tense silence. He was asked what his profession had been before the war to which he replied 'undertaker' and was promptly marched off to the cells amid laughter and cheering.

Early in 1944 the British identified a 'stool pigeon' in their midst; Lieutenant Walter Purdy, a former junior mechanic in the Merchant Navy who had been pressed into service as an officer with the Royal Navy at the outbreak of war. His ship was sunk off Norway and he was captured, but prison life was not an existence that he was prepared to accept or tolerate and he was soon speaking openly about his desire to see a fascist government in England, and that Britain was not only weak but heading for defeat. He was quickly identified by the Germans as a potential collaborator who could be infiltrated into a prison camp to gather information on escape lines in occupied Europe and thus, in March 1940, he arrived in Colditz using the alias 'Bob Poynter'. Those already in the castle were always wary of new arrivals until, or unless, they were able to vouch for themselves, but Purdy's particular misfortune was to be identified as a German sympathizer by Captain Julius Green, then in Colditz but formerly the dental officer at a number of other camps – including Marlag, where Merchant Navy seamen were imprisoned in the early years of the war.[2] Regrettably, before Green saw him, Purdy had been warmly welcomed by some of the officers and while being shown around the castle had seen some tunnellers at work, as well as the hide where they secreted their tools. Recognised and exposed by Julius Green he was interrogated by Lieutenant Colonel George Young, Security Officer for the British, and quickly broke down, making a full confession. The SBO, Colonel Willy Tod, immediately informed the Germans that unless Purdy was removed from the camp his safety could not be guaranteed, but some of the British had already decided to take matters into their own hands. Plans were made to hang him but when the moment came, nobody could be found who was willing to carry out the execution and Purdy was removed by the Germans to broadcast propaganda from Berlin after having spent just three days in the castle. Purdy was prosecuted after the war and sentenced to death for working with the Germans, but the sentence was commuted to life imprisonment of which he served eight years before being released. Both hides he had seen were raided by the Germans shortly after his departure.

Even senior German officers were not spared the attentions of the prisoners and learned to be cautious when in the castle. On one occasion a visiting General pledged to try and improve their conditions 'if there was a bit of give and take', citing as an example the necessity of saluting German officers whatever their rank. A number of apparently curious prisoners gathered around him asking questions that he answered with courtesy and good humour until, realising his hat, baton and briefcase had disappeared, he threatened dire consequences if they were not returned within ten minutes. The briefcase that had been lifted was rushed to the prisoners' quarters where it was opened and the contents, an invaluable assortment of travel documents used in the Reich by foreign and domestic workers, was photographed. It was then returned locked and intact, apparently untouched, along with the General's baton and hat. No further action was taken by the no-doubt embarrassed General.

Getting out of Colditz was, however, only the first step in achieving a 'home run'. The escapee had to reach a neutral country and declare himself to the authorities, preferably the British Consulate if there was one. This was recognised by the War Office and in December 1939 a new and secret department, MI9, was created to assist Allied POWs in their escape efforts. An early decision was taken by MI9 to send maps of areas which they believed those escaping would be most likely to cross. In the case of occupied Europe, they chose the borders with Switzerland and Spain, and the areas of ports where shipping from neutral companies docked to unload. It was decided that maps should be printed on silk, more flexible and durable than paper and noiseless when hidden about one's person. They persuaded the manufacturers of leisure items such as board games, playing cards, chess sets, gramophone records, dart boards, table tennis and cricket bats, to help them by hiding the maps inside such items during their manufacture. Escape compasses were the next important piece of equipment to be developed by MI9 and were sent to camps in many different ways hidden in uniforms, in buttons or inside innocent looking everyday items. An example is the 'swinger compass' made from small magnetised strips of diamond-shaped steel sheet with three small holes, two at one end filled with luminous paint held in place with varnish to indicate north, and a smaller hole at the other, southern, end; in the centre another hole enabled the compass to be suspended on a piece of string. They were basic but easy to conceal and remarkably accurate.

A particular security concern for the Germans lay within their regular camp staff, especially those who had been there a while and had become familiar with the prisoners habits and routines; the better they got to know the prisoners the more susceptible they became to bribery with cigarettes, chocolate or coffee, and the insidious effects of familiarity and simple politeness between themselves and the prisoners on the diligence with which they carried out their duties. The guards were all known to the prisoners by nickname:

> There was Cheese – he was a little man – what we (Germans) call 'three cheeses high' (Dreikäsehoch); the Policeman; Hiawatha, who rather fancied himself until he discovered that his mate was known as Minnehaha; Big Bum; Auntie, the Quartermaster who was in Colditz right to the end; Fouine, the French word for ferret, known to the English as Dixon Hawke, very clever at smelling out tunnels; and Mussolini, our staff sergeant in charge of the orderlies, an old soldier from the first war who disliked all officers, even his own![3]

As an officers' prison camp, Colditz was more comfortable than many *Kriegsgefangen offiziers sonderlager,* food was plentiful, morale high and the German parcels' staff were honest; despite the shortages, and often complete absence, in the Reich of luxuries such as coffee, chocolate, jam, cigarettes and tobacco, Red Cross parcels were not pilfered. Prisoners organised themselves into 'messes' to supplement the issued German rations: 'Our German rations apart from the bread which, although made from rye, was quite palatable were as bad as ever. The Concise Oxford Dictionary describes rye as cereal used for bread in northern Continental countries and for fodder in UK.'

The camp was relatively comfortable with two-tiered bunks, straw palliasses and sheets, many of which disappeared to be used as makeshift ropes while the wooden slats on the bunks were often taken to shore up tunnels that were being dug, leaving officers in danger of falling through their beds onto the floor or the unfortunate occupant of a lower bunk.

As officers were not required to work they had plenty of time to study the routine of those guarding them and identify any routines or patterns of behaviour that might be exploited to break out of the castle. Not all of those in Colditz were looking to escape, but all were willing to help facilitate and support attempts by others using what skills they already had or had developed. Officers became adept at forgery, tailoring, crafting dummy weapons and German military accoutrements. Many hours of observation and planning went into any scheme submitted to the Escape Committee and at this Mike excelled.

CHAPTER 11

THE LIGHT WELL

In November 1942 Mike, after only eight months in Colditz, made his first attempt to escape from the castle with a fellow prisoner, Captain Charles Klein, an officer in the French elite specialist mountain warfare troops the '67 Chasseur Alpin'. These troops had been sent to Norway in early April 1940 following the German attack and invasion as part of a combined British and French force to secure resources, in particular the minerals and iron ore that were vital to the Allied war effort. Germany sought to secure naval bases in Norway for operations against the British fleet in the North Sea and to ensure the supply of iron-ore shipments from neutral Sweden that were vital to German industry. Controlling Norway would also give access to the Atlantic Ocean allowing Germany to use sea power effectively against the Allies and enabling reconnaissance aircraft to operate far over the North Atlantic. U-boats and surface ships operating out of Norwegian naval bases would also be able to break the blockade line across the North Sea and attack convoys heading to Great Britain. The fighting in Norway took place in severe cold and snow on both land and at sea until by late May 1940, despite a few hard-won breakthroughs, the Allied situation became untenable and it was decided to withdraw the Allied troops.

Charles Klein arrived at Colditz with Lieutenant Desjobert, who had been the leader of an unsuccessful escape in Poland on the eve of the Operation Barbarossa, an interesting coincidence to Mike's on the spot or deported to a concentration camp. The longer they remained at large, the more determined the Germans would become to uncover how they had been helped – perhaps even resorting to torture if their captives revealed nothing. Their decision was to place their trust in Mrs M and Puffy, who were caring for them with great dedication. Even so, the constant fear of discovery – and of the entire family being arrested – haunted them, making this a time of relentless strain and anxiety.

Towards the middle of August, Mike, Ronnie, and Gris met in the flat that Mrs M had made her headquarters to hear of a plan to get four Polish officers to Turkey via Budapest. The route involved travelling by train to Cracow and from there being guided over the mountains into Slovakia, where they would be met and driven to the Hungarian border. A guide would take them across, after which they were to make their own way by train to Budapest, where friends would be waiting. There was room for only one extra traveller, but after much persuasion the Poles agreed to stand down one of their party and take two of the British. Ronnie, as the senior, and Mike, as the linguist, were the obvious choices, so Gris stepped aside to await the next opportunity.

Shortly afterwards, the woman organising the escape arrived, followed at intervals by a member of the local Underground and the three Poles who would make the journey. Mike sat down with them and went over the plan meticulously before agreeing that they should depart at the end of the month.

Duly, on the evening of 26 August, Ronnie, Mike, and the three Poles boarded a train to Kraków, where they spent the night. Around 3 pm the following afternoon, they caught another train to Zakopane, in the far south of the country near the Slovak border. They disembarked in a small village a few miles northeast of the town at about nine that evening, where they met another Pole who was to be their guide. After a meal, they walked through the night to a second village, northwest of Zakopane, where they rested the following day, planning to move on after dark and cross the frontier into Slovakia. As night fell, they were picked up by a car and driven 140 kilometres to the outskirts of Rožňava, then walked a short distance to meet a second car that took them to a railway station south of the town. The Poles purchased the tickets, and at 9 pm, on 31 August, they boarded a train bound for Budapest.

The departure of Mike and Ronnie left Gris facing the prospect of the coming winter alone – awaiting news of their progress and moving frequently for security. Time passed, and as winter closed in, there was still no word from them. Warsaw looked picturesque under the snow, but with fuel scarce and the high cost of food driving a flourishing black market, the cold brought great hardship to many Poles. Gris settled into a quiet routine, spending his nights in an empty flat belonging to a friend of Puffy. His days passed pleasantly enough – reading, listening to the radio, and studying to improve his German – but still there was no news of Ronnie or Mike. At last, word came that they had completed the first stage of their journey and had arrived safely in Budapest. Yet this good news was overshadowed by disappointment: the arrangements that had been made for Gris to follow them had collapsed. There was nothing he could do but swallow his frustration and continue to wait – hoping each day for the call to join them.

Several weeks passed, and Gris grew increasingly anxious that his continued presence in Warsaw was putting those helping him in danger of discovery. At the same time, he knew that setting out without proper plans or preparation – and being caught – would risk interrogation, under which he might break down and reveal everything. On balance, and despite his fears, he decided that his best course was to remain in Warsaw, alongside the growing number of escaped prisoners of all ranks being sheltered by the Polish Underground. After Christmas, to fill his days, he became involved with the Polish Home Army in the production and circulation of a covert newspaper. It was shortly afterwards that he heard news of two British officers – *"one a major,* experience with Gris and Ronnie. His first impressions were of the contrasts between the gloomy fortress and the pleasant surroundings in which it sat, the oppressive constant surveillance and the irrepressible nature of the imprisoned officers. Colditz society was characterised by youth, insolence, and the prisoners desire to escape';[1] it was a highly competitive business between nationalities, escape teams and even friends. When a number of officers were relocated to Oflag X-C he was moved into a new room shared with a fellow Officer, Aulaid, also from the Chasseur Alpin. Together they looked at potential escape routes from the castle and after a while identified the possibility of using an abandoned lift shaft that ran from a large room known as 'the Theatre'. Looking down the shaft they were able to see a tiled surface several floors below from where they could hear the sound of pots and pans banging together; knowing they were not above the prisoners' kitchen that opened onto the inner courtyard they assessed the noises could only have come from the German garrison kitchen that gave access to the area beyond the walls of the castle. After days of covert surveillance the route they were hoping to use seemed impossible; the theatre was checked regularly and at the same time the security bars on the lift shaft were examined for any sign of tampering. They were on the verge of giving up when they realised that on certain days there was a break, usually around midday, between the arrival of the cooks and the guards coming on duty; it was during this gap that they worked, cutting through the bars with a razor blade notched like a saw, a long slow job but with the advantage that the resultant cut was very thin and could be concealed by filling it with the soft centre from one of the loaves issued to them daily.

It was not long, however, before the activity was noticed by the British, who invited Klein to a meeting in one of their rooms at which they proposed a joint French/British operation; they would supply the rope and German army uniforms and in return two officers, Rupert Barry and Mike, would join the French team; the proposal was accepted and preparations went ahead. By now it was autumn and there was a feeling that they needed to hurry as the cuts in the security bars deepened and became increasingly hard to conceal, but misfortune struck when their carefully made uniforms and cord were found and lifted during a routine search. It was not until 25 November that their losses were made good and they returned to the theatre ready to try again. The four escapees had drawn lots to decide their order of departure; Mike was to go first followed by Klein, Aulaid was third and then Barry. The partially sawn-through bars were forced open; the cord securely tied to the lift security bar and the end tossed into the shaft. Klein recalled:

> Sinclair threw off his trench coat, put on his German forage cap, gripped the cord and disappeared. A few seconds later I received the signal … and slid down the rope to the tiles of the kitchen whereupon, looking up, I saw Sinclair face to face with a dumbfounded German cook.[2]

Mike and Klein quickly walked past the bemused cook to the door opening onto the spiral staircase that led to the outer German courtyard and began to descend it. On the way down they passed a German officer climbing the stairs whom, with great presence of mind, they both saluted; moments later Klein opened a door on the staircase that revealed a German NCO snoozing on his bed and quickly closed it again. As planned, they exited into the courtyard that they knew was on the route to the prisoners' exercise area. They headed for the gate and sentry post that guarded access to the park realising as they drew close to it that neither of them knew the password. Luck was with them and the sentry did not challenge them as they passed and calmly continued on their way to the park. The high brick wall on the edge of the exercise area looked daunting but did not prove to be a major obstacle and they both scrambled over it; Mike slipped on landing and rolled to the bottom of the gulley but was unhurt. Together they set off at the double through the woods trying to put as much distance between themselves and the castle as possible, pausing from time to time to listen for any sounds of pursuit. After several hundred yards, with no sound of followers or the alarm being raised, they halted to strip off their German uniforms revealing Mike in civilian clothing and Klein disguised as a French prisoner of war employed as a farm labourer. They marched all night through woods and sleeping villages trying to put as much distance between themselves and the castle as possible until at sunrise, wishing each other well, they separated to take their chances individually.

Klein was soon arrested trying to pass himself off as one of the French prisoners working on a nearby farm; he gave his captors the slip a few days later but was again unlucky and arrested at Plauen railway station with a ticket to Nuremberg in his pocket. He was taken to the local police station and then to the local prison where his true identity was soon discovered and he was returned to Colditz. Mike was on the run for longer and managed to get close to freedom, being caught several days later near Tuttlingen in the frontier zone when he took a chance and walked over a bridge rather than look for a suitable spot to wade or swim across the river. Being close to the Swiss frontier he ought to have anticipated that the bridge would be guarded, but cold, hunger and thirst – or perhaps over confidence in his linguistic ability to pass as a German, impaired his judgement.

Unbeknown to them, Barry and Aulaid had not been able to follow as they had intended. Just as they were preparing to descend the lift shaft several German soldiers appeared in the Theatre having been ordered to carry out a security 'spot check' of the room, forcing them to remain hidden until the check was complete. By the time the soldiers left, the window of opportunity had passed and reluctantly they had to stand down. On trying again the next day, 26 November, and successfully descending to the German kitchen and exiting into the courtyard, they made their way to the gate leading to the park.

On reaching it, in marked contrast to the experience of Mike and Klein the day before, the sentry asked to check their passes. Unable to produce any they were arrested. Aulaid was identified almost immediately, but Barry had shaved off his distinctive moustache and it was a while before he was recognised.

There is no record of how long a prison sentence the escapees received on return to Colditz, but it is certain they would have been given a period of solitary confinement, probably thirty days. It is equally as certain that Mike will not have spent time in self-recrimination over his bad fortune in being arrested so near to success, he will have devoted it instead to analysing what had gone wrong, the mistakes he had made and how to profit from the experience in the planning and execution of another attempt once he had been released from solitary. While taking a parole walk in the park an idea came to him sparked by the escape of Mairesse-LeBrun, who had made a 'home run' some fifteen months before. Prisoners marched down to the park under escort, but once there were left to their own devices with only a few guards outside the perimeter wire while the prisoners played football, strolled around or sat quietly enjoying being out of the claustrophobic surroundings of the castle. After mulling over his idea and assessing the chances of success Mike felt confident enough to discuss it with Gris.

His idea was to cut through the wire fence that ran around the walk area and head off through the adjacent woodland; it was a simple plan, often the most likely to succeed. Covertly cutting an exit hole in the wire would take some weeks if they were to avoid drawing attention to themselves and possibly suspicion, by going to the park together too frequently. The plan was to sit leaning their backs against the fence as if relaxing while taking turns to use a saw held under the arm to cut the outline of a panel through which they could exit; it would take some weeks. When the panel was almost complete they would join a walk and finish it off, crawl up the bramble covered bank on that side of the park and slip over the wall to freedom hoping to be away 45 minutes before the end of walk head count. Sadly, when sawing was almost complete the Germans found the cut in the fence and replaced that area of the panel.

It was another disappointment for Mike and once again he was sentenced to a period of solitary confinement, but he remained undeterred and on release it was not long before he spotted another opportunity for escape. He suffered from chronic sinusitis, a permanent condition, and in early 1943 was taken under escort to a hospital in Leipzig for treatment. The journey involved a short eight-minute walk from the castle to the railway station and a train journey of around ninety minutes to Leipzig; on arrival there it was another short escorted walk to the hospital. His first visit for treatment gave him the opportunity to assess the possibility it offered for escape and what preparation he would need to make if it seemed favourable; in effect it became a reconnaissance for another attempt to get away. On 12 June 1943, on a second visit for dental treatment, he slipped out of the hospital and away into the city. There is no record of how he did this, but he must have worn his battledress to travel to the hospital and been able to make some superficial alterations and additions to 'civilianise' it.

On 16 June, 250 miles away in Cologne, he was stopped following a heavy air raid and questioned by the local *Ordnungspolizei*, the Civil Police, looking for any bomber crewmen who had bailed out of damaged aircraft. His disguise and story failed and he was returned to Colditz. There is no record of any punishment received, but without doubt he would have been sentenced to solitary confinement, most probably for thirty days – the longest period that could be imposed without the formality of a court martial. Again, Mike would have used the time to mull over the attempt and draw lessons for future plans.

CHAPTER 12

FELDWEBEL ROTHENBERG

Mike's next attempt to break out – and his and the most audacious yet – was in September 1943. The German Guard Company in Colditz numbered around 165 five officers, NCOs and soldiers divided into the platoons that provided the daily guard rotas. The SNCO in charge of Number 3 Platoon of the Guard Company was *Stabsfeldwebel* Rothenberger, a sergeant major, who wore several First World War decorations including the Iron Cross (First Class). He was 60 years old and known to the prisoners as 'Franz Joseph' on account of his most noticeable physical feature, a huge 'Hindenburg' moustache, ginger with grey tips and always immaculately clipped in the regulation manner that mirrored the style of the former Austro-Hungarian Emperor Franz Joseph; aside from the moustache, his physical similarity to Mike in height, build and colouring was remarkable; all that was needed to turn Mike into *Stabsfeldwebel* Rothenberger, apart from a uniform and accoutrements, was a little greying of the hair and a large false moustache. Mike studied the German routine for posting and relieving sentries and after several weeks had worked out an ambitious idea involving himself as 'Franz Joseph' and two other prisoners, suitably dressed and equipped, as soldiers from *Stabsfeldwebel* Rothenberger's Guard Platoon.

In outline, the plan was to disguise the red-headed Mike as Rothenberger and then for him, as the *stabsfeldwebel*, to relieve the two sentries covering the route that led around the castle to the park, replacing them with two suitably disguised prisoners. Once done, and with the two German sentries on their way back to the guardroom, Mike, in the role of Rothenberger, would make his way to the third sentry who was positioned guarding the gate leading to the park. The escape by Pat Reid and others the previous year had used this route, so the sentry was now posted on a specially constructed catwalk above the gate, giving him sight into what had been dead ground previously; however, if he too could be sent back to the guard room, a route out of the castle grounds and into the surrounding countryside would be opened for Mike and his two 'sentries'.

The plan was approved by the Escape Committee and two other prisoners, Lance Pope and John Hyde-Thomson, were selected as the sentries to be posted as 'reliefs' by Mike in his role as 'Franz Joseph'. Preparations were detailed and thorough; Mike studied Rothenberger's speech, accent, mannerisms and walk over a period of four weeks, dogging his footsteps whenever he entered the prisoners' courtyard. Uniforms, rifles for the two guards and a holster and pistol for Mike, or at the least the butt protruding from the holster, were needed, the latter requiring detailed work and particular accuracy as it would be seen close up, albeit in semi-darkness, by the three guards being relieved.[1] Rothenberger's carefully trimmed ginger coloured 'Hindenburg' moustache, complete with grey tips, was another challenge to be met as it too would be seen at close quarters when Mike spoke to and relieved the three guards, but on the plus side – it would cover much of Mike's face and features greatly enhancing his disguise.

Rothenberger was followed whenever he set foot in the prisoners' courtyard and his mannerisms, demeanour and bearing observed closely by Mike and others. The task of creating a moustache was undertaken by Teddy Barton, one of several prisoners who had settled into the role of putting on theatre productions and found that he had a gift and professional touch for making up individuals; he made fourteen moustaches before he was satisfied that he had the right one. Uniforms were another challenge but there was some expertise among the prisoners in making them as at least five escapes had already taken place in which one or more individuals had been dressed as Germans. Tailoring and dying was soon underway using whatever cloth could be acquired, while two others were taken into the plan and commissioned to provide the necessary accoutrements and firearms: two German rifles, two bayonet scabbards, a revolver, or at least a realistic butt, and holster, buttons, badges, medals and belt clasps had to be created.

If all went according to plan there would be an opportunity for others to break out in the gap between the third sentry arriving at the guardroom, seeing his Guard Commander there and, realising that it was not Rothenberger who had relieved him, rushing back to his post to apprehend the individual impersonating the *stabsfeldwebel*. In anticipation of the possibility for a mass breakout, alongside the rehearsals and preparations for Mike's attempt, materials in the form of papers, rations, maps and money were assembled for twenty others hoping to escape, a major undertaking for those with the necessary skills. The intention was that after the evening 'Appel', when the prisoners had returned to their rooms and settled down, those hoping to take the opportunity of getting away would quietly make their way to their respective hides where their 'civilian' clothes and escape material were concealed. They would get dressed ready to go and make their way through several rooms, unlocking the doors with specially made keys, and prepare to make the rope descent onto the path to the park. Once the guards had been relieved and were out of sight on their way back to the guard room, the waiting officers would make their descent and head straight for the park, followed by Mike and his two sentries. Instructions were to keep moving and ignore any Germans they came across, leaving 'Franz Joseph' to order them to go back to the Guard Room and raise the alarm while he himself and his two sentries continued the pursuit.

The attempt was to be made on 2 September when Rothenberg was scheduled to be the Guard Commander and an especially dumb-looking individual was calculated to be posted overlooking the park gate. With the final bar cutting on the window completed and camouflaged, an air of enforced casualness concealed the excitement and nervous tension of those waiting. After the evening roll call at 9 pm when all was quiet, Mike and his two sentries moved off to the sick ward while stooges took up their respective positions, one group to overlook the guardhouse while another led the main escape party through the locked doors of the old, now empty, British quarters. Reports began to come in:

'The ivory headed Goon is at his post' …
'Franz Joseph returned to Guardhouse' …
'All quiet in Guardhouse'…

This last report would be the signal for Mike and his two 'sentries' to clamber down the rope and onto the path around the castle. It was about midnight as they went out of the sick bay window and marched to the first sentry: '*Sie sind abgelöst. Sie werden Ihre Wache diesem Posten übergeben. Gehen Sie so fort in die Wachstube. Dort sind Sie nötig denn einige Gefangene sind geflohen.*' (You are relieved. You will hand over your duties at this post. Go to the guardroom at once. You are needed there, some prisoners have escaped.)

The sentry obeyed and Lance Pope was put in his place. The second sentry was replaced by John Hyde-Thomson, but instead of setting off to the guard room waited for his friend on the bridge to be relieved and join him. Mike climbed onto the catwalk where the guard roster had posted an individual known to the prisoners as the 'ivory headed goon'. When he was spoken to by 'Franz Joseph' he handed over his keys and set off but then, for no reason he could later explain, thought better of it and asked Franz Joseph for his pass. Reflecting on the incident subsequently, the guard stated that when

'Franz Joseph' approached he did not look over both sides of the catwalk as he usually did and aroused his suspicion. *'Bist du doof? Kennst du nicht deinen eigenen Stabsfeldwebel?'* (Are you daft? Don't you know your own Sergeant Major?)

But the sentry remained suspicious and telling Mike to stay where he was shouted to his friend to sound the alarm while covering Mike with his rifle. *Obergefreiter* (Corporal) Pilz appeared on the scene with a drawn revolver, followed shortly thereafter by two more groups of Germans. The officer in charge of one group seemed over excited, more intent on inflaming the situation than taking command. He drew his pistol and seemed keen to use it, which contributed to the excitement; he screamed: 'Hands up!' 'My hands are up!' came the reply.

Pilz then repeatedly shouted a word which Mike did not understand, but said later sounded like *'abschnallen'*, disarm yourself, before he fired. It is not clear why he fired; although the situation was confused it was within the camp perimeter, the area was well lit and Mike was clearly not a threat, standing with his hands raised in an attitude of surrender.

The bullet struck Mike in the left side, travelled through his chest and exited on the right without hitting any vital organs. He fell to his knees where he remained for several minutes before being ordered to move off. He replied: '*Wie kann ich, wenn ich durch die Brust geschossen wurde?*' (How can I when I have been shot through the chest?)

But no help came and he had to make his way slowly and painfully to the guardroom unaided, while from the many watching at the Castle windows there were angry shouts of 'German murderers'.

The escape attempt had failed, but by how small a margin. Mike recovered quickly, was back from hospital in two days and after a period of punishment was already thinking about his next attempt to escape.

CHAPTER 13

ACROSS THE TERRACE

Despite the disappointment he must have felt at failing so close to success, Mike remained determined to breakout of Colditz and return to active service; he firmly believed it was his duty and he was not prepared to sit back and await liberation. Now he studied the guard routines day and night in a manner that could only be described as obsessive, looking for any pattern that might be exploited to offer a chance of getting away. By now every potential escape route had been used, many of them a number of times, but after four months watching from a window 30ft above the terrace Mike realised that nobody had tried the north-west corner of the castle where, once across the narrow path patrolled by a sentry along the foot of the outer wall, the ground fell away in a precipice to open country.

The Germans also studied each escape attempt and the route taken, they too had noted that the north-west side of the castle remained untried and concluded it was an escape route that must have been disregarded by the prisoners as impossible so needed no increase in guards. Nevertheless, acknowledging the ingenuity of the prisoners, they occasionally altered the sentries' routine to avoid establishing any pattern in the area that might be identified and exploited. The study Mike made of the changing day to night sentry positions on the north and west sides of the castle lasted for six months, concentrating on the half hour before and after the flood lights were switched on;

it revealed that as darkness fell and it became increasingly difficult to see their areas of responsibility, it had become the practice for sentries to leave their posts to cover their arcs from the garden area at the north-west foot of the castle walls until they were relieved by the night shift. Instructions from Berlin to save electricity directed that the perimeter search lights would not be switched on until a minute after dark, providing a brief opportunity for escape; it did not happen every evening – but often enough to make it worth trying. After working out the details and timings Mike approached the Escape Committee with his proposal, they listened and gave him their full support. As his plan was for two people Mike spoke to Gris about joining him; Gris was delighted and agreed without hesitation, only to be bitterly disappointed when the Escape Committee intervened to direct that Jack Best[1] should be given a chance after spending nearly a year as one of the two 'ghosts' concealed within the castle.

The idea of 'ghosts' came from the Escape Committee, who had decided that parading for roll calls four times a day, as the officers were required to do, slowed progress too much when they were tunnelling. Their solution was to create a couple of extra bodies to stand in on roll calls and enable those digging to work on without interruption. Two officers, Jack Best and Mike Harvey, a submariner captured in January 1940, volunteered for the role and went into hiding during the commotion and parades to check numbers following the capture of a Dutch officer attempting to escape. After counting, and counting again, the Germans were satisfied that not one, but two, prisoners were missing and assumed that while three had been involved in the escape only one had been caught. Work on the tunnel had stopped during these 'Appels', and it was discovered by the Germans soon after, but by then the Escape Committee had realised how useful extra bodies would be in covering for those on the run and so, for nearly a year, Best and Harvey became 'ghosts' haunting the castle, living in cupboards and under floorboards. For several months they only came out for an hour in the evenings to wash and eat, did not receive or send any mail and did not venture into the prisoners' yard but, as their confidence grew, they would sometimes sleep in a prisoner's bed while that individual took a turn as 'a ghost', concealed away. After three months, seeing that the Guard force personnel had been changed and new prisoners had arrived, Best and Harvey felt it safe to appear more frequently and, confident enough to make up numbers when men were stuck in a tunnel unable to get back for a roll call – or even occasionally to borrow a uniform and join new arrivals to go for a walk. However, despite these interludes it remained a tense existence, always ready to run and hide in an instant and never able to spend long enough in the fresh air to lose the pallor of their long absence from daylight.

Now that Best had had been nominated to accompany Mike they both needed to gather suitable civilian clothing or borrow items from fellow prisoners. For Mike there was a decent suit, overcoat and hat available that fitted well; Best was lent a naval uniform and once clear of the castle, he would remove the braid and pull off the naval buttons to reveal round black buttons (fashioned from old gramophone records) underneath – the uniform then made a decent civilian suit.[2] He made himself a black coat to prevent the suit from getting muddy during the escape; it would get torn badly, but served its purpose well.

Arse creepers[3] were issued to each of them in which to conceal money and tracings of the area where they planned to cross the Dutch frontier. Best recalled in later life that on his escape he was very thankful to be able to remove it after three weeks when finally clear of the castle. They were also given counterfeit official identification passes complete with photographs taken using a homemade camera, developed and cut to size which they decided to keep on them rather than risk disfiguring by trying to hide them away. They were also issued with a briefcase in which to carry some food, a change of socks and wire cutters made for them by one of the back-room helpers and were to be discarded after they had got through the second fence.

Dark balaclavas covered their heads, and socks over their shoes deadened their footsteps; as far as possible nothing was left to chance but despite careful planning and preparation small things could still be missed; it was not until they were on the run that Best noticed the locks on his briefcase had 'Made in England' stamped on them.

The pair practised their escape in a circular stairwell by throwing down a 'rope' made from bed sheets knotted together and using a board as a platform, launching themselves after it through an improvised 'hole' exactly matching the one to be cut in the window bars, Mike opting to go out feet first, Best, head first. Nothing was left to chance as the pair went over the plan and rehearsed their exit from the castle again and again.

On 18 January 1944 they were ready to make their attempt – but that night the perimeter lights came on immediately darkness fell, and although the sentries had moved to ground level as expected, the attempt was aborted and everything returned to hides. It was a disappointment, but not a disaster, and all preparations were made for another attempt the next night, 19 January. This time, as twilight turned to dusk and night fell, the perimeter lights did not come on immediately, leaving the north-west corner temporarily in darkness and, as anticipated, hidden from both sentries. Neither Mike nor Best were aware as they exited the castle that they had narrowly avoided being discovered when German workmen appeared to repair a lavatory cistern that Best had reported as broken some time earlier.

Mike was first to be launched out of the window, swiftly descending the 90ft of bed sheets to the terrace and across it, securing the end of the rope he was carrying to the balustrade before throwing the rest over and setting off down it with Best following seconds later. In clambering over the balustrade one of them must have pressed an alarm bell missed during their meticulous study of the area; as they reached the ground and tugged on the rope, the signal for it to be pulled up, the guard room door opened and one of the guards stepped out just before the perimeter lights came on. Leaving a brightly lit room for darkness, the guard did not see the first rope being whipped back up, or detect Mike cutting the wire below; the second rope length was out of sight from the guardroom and not found until the next day.

Mike and Best scrambled down the slope, across a barbed-wire concertina entanglement and into the back yard of a cottage just as a woman opened her window and looked out; fortunately for them, seeing all was quiet up at the castle, she took no more interest and closed it again. Unobserved they brushed themselves down and quickly tidied their appearance before walking over the River Mulde bridge and into a wood, where they stopped to repair their clothes managing to thread a needle and stitch up the tears by the light of a cigarette. Best's overcoat was, however, so badly ripped that they ran out of thread before they had closed all the tears and had to resort to safety pins to hold the rest together. Despite his concerns over 'Made in England' being stamped on the locks, Best used his briefcase to cover the repairs and took the opportunity to civilianise' his uniform underneath by removing and burying the naval buttons and braid.

The two were now ready to set off, navigating across country by compass, aiming to catch a train from Grimma eight miles away. In Colditz a railway timetable had been acquired by bribing a guard, and this enabled them to plan their arrival time to buy tickets and board a train promptly, avoiding the risk of drawing attention to themselves as they waited on the platform. In the dark they walked into several fences but reached the station on schedule, where nobody took any interest in them and there were no police to be seen. Mike bought two tickets to Eilenburg, giving one to Best so they could travel independently but in the same compartment and in sight of each other. They left the train before it reached Leipzig, some thirty kilometres from Eilenburg, believing that their absence from Colditz must have been discovered by then and the police in the city alerted, but after a short uneventful wait they were able to take a further train to Eilenburg, where it stopped around midnight.

Their priority was to distance themselves from the castle, so they left the town and, using their compass, set off to walk sixteen miles to Bitterfeld to catch another train; hiding in the roadside ditch as the occasional car passed, they arrived in the town at 5.30 in the morning, just as people began to stir. It took them an hour to find the station as they did not want to risk arousing interest or curiosity by asking for directions, leaving them just enough time to buy tickets and board a train for Magdeburg – but they soon realised that the station direction signs had been incorrect and they did not know where they were headed. Thanks to Mike's ability to speak Polish, albeit limited, he discovered they were on a train carrying Poles to work; heeding their advice they jumped off the train and laid low in some woods. After a short wait to be certain they had not been spotted they set off back to Bitterfeld,

They had decided to travel on the slow trains as the railway police usually inspected passes on the fast ones. They had a long wait before another arrived and they were again on the move. By midnight they were getting close to Osnabruck when an air raid damaged the line ahead making it impassable; with typical German efficiency buses were provided and passengers, most of whom were military, or at least wearing uniforms, were allocated to them. Feeling conspicuous as the only civilians who would be on the bus to which they were directed, they decided instead to walk the remaining distance to Osnabruck. They arrived tired and bad tempered, just in time to catch the first train going west. They got off at Rheine thirty miles further on, checked trains to their next destination, Bentheim twenty-two miles west on the Dutch frontier, and then left the station to find a quiet spot and make a plan.

Wanting to have as long a period of darkness as possible to cross the frontier they decided to catch a train that would arrive at Bentheim, thirty minutes away, soon after dusk fell at around 5 pm. It was only a short 30 minute trip, so with at least six hours to wait before they needed to set off they settled down under a hedge for a rest. For Best the respite was welcome; he was suffering from sore feet and blisters, partly from lack of exercise while a ghost in Colditz, but mostly because his shoes were too small; he had worked through the pain they were causing him and managed to walk without limping to avoid attracting attention and unwelcome interest that might easily have unmasked him.

Refreshed after a few hours, and feeling hungry, having already finished the food they had, they walked back to Rheine and were able to enjoy some ration free soup and beer at an inn. They still had some hours to wait so went to a cinema hoping to be warm and comfortable, possibly to sleep, but they were not allowed in because the film had started. Some soldiers who had also been refused entry were kicking up a fuss about it, so to avoid being dragged into the row they hurried away and began to walk about the town trying to look purposeful but unwittingly paused outside a police station. Bests' very pale appearance aroused curiosity from one individual there:

'Woher kommen Sie?' (Where are you from?)mmm.

'Von Leipzig.' (From Leipzig.)

Clearly unsatisfied, and with one hand in his pocket that they presumed held a pistol, he retorted: '*Kommen Sie mit*.' (Come with me.)

He ordered them into a building where they were pushed into a room and forced to strip. Mike's pass was soon found and with delight declared to be a forgery; Best was asked for his and, while rummaging through his pockets to find it, succeeded in crumpling up and eating two tracings he was carrying of the Dutch frontier.

However, what the police had found was sufficient to send them to a concentration camp so they admitted to being escaped British prisoners of war. At once the police relaxed and became almost friendly; they were put in a cell for the night and, seeing blood stains on the walls and filthy mattresses caked in blood on the floor, were grateful that they had declared their status. Mike, suffering from nervous exhaustion, went straight to sleep despite the conditions.

In the morning, they were given a meal before being collected by an NCO and four German soldiers; as they set off, one of the police ran after them with a bill for their 'bed and breakfast', but they were already on their way and it remained unpaid. Their destination was a French prisoner of war camp close to the Dutch border where they spent two nights in the cells before being collected by guards from Colditz and taken back to the castle. It was yet another disappointment for Mike who became dejected and withdrawn, his depression made worse by news that his younger brother John, serving with the Scots Guards, had been killed at Anzio. Gris noticed how he would bite through his pipe stem, almost a monthly occurrence, but all attempts to draw close to him were rebuffed.

CHAPTER 14

A HOME RUN

The final attempted escape and death of 'The Red Fox', his funeral and burial service.

In the aftermath of the mass escape attempt from Stalag Luft III on the night 24/25 March 1944 by seventy-seven Allied airmen,[1] the German authorities issued an official warning on 23 July addressed 'To all Prisoners of War' beginning with: 'The escape from prison camps is no longer a sport!' And to emphasise the point ending with: 'Escaping from prison camps has ceased to be a sport!'

This took time to filter down the chain of command and it was not until 23 September that it had been distributed and the full text placed on notice boards in Colditz stating: 'Anyone engaged in non-military gangster war will be shot on sight. To avoid such an occurrence all prisoners should stay in their camps and refrain from any attempt to escape.'

Despite this warning most in Colditz continued to see it as their duty to escape, although Colonel Willy Tod, the Commandant, said he would only approve future attempts if he and the Escape Committee believed they had a real chance of success.

On 28 August Mike, planning another escape attempt, joined the daily exercise party and walked down to the park wearing civilian clothes underneath his uniform. He was planning to scale the wire, as had been done successfully before, but his bad luck persisted, his extra clothes were spotted by one of the guards and he was sentenced to fourteen days solitary confinement going into the cells on 4 September. Thinking of climbing the park wire fence in broad daylight may appear to border on the amateur compared with the elaborate nature of his earlier attempts but as a successful escape had been made from the park by Mariesse-LeBrun, it was still considered a vulnerable area in the castle's security. On the 1 September 1944, Mike's great friend Ronnie Littledale, with whom he had been involved in several attempts to escape and who had made a home run from Colditz, had been killed in Normandy. It is not clear when this news reached Mike, but it will have been soon after the event and will certainly have had a profound effect on him, particularly following the death of his younger brother. It was the firm opinion of those who knew Mike well that he remained desperate to make it back to England 'to do his bit before it was all over', and that this was what drove him on despite his long list of near successes and disappointments.

On 25 September, a week after his release from solitary, Mike was again assembling with other officers preparing to walk down to the park wearing a large French khaki coat about his shoulders. Gris, seeing him fully clad in his French overcoat and alone, guessed something was afoot, although Mike had never hinted that he had any plan, and so approached him:

> 'Hello Mike, I see you're going on the walk would you like a bit of company?'
>
> 'I'd rather go alone thank you.'

Gris persisted but got another equally flat rejection after which he gave up and walked off, somewhat irritated and with no idea that Mike was getting ready to make another attempt to break out of the castle. Kenneth Lockwood,[2] the Treasurer for the British Escape Committee in Colditz, whom Mike had approached for money from the escape fund – which he was given without any questions asked – was the only person who had an inkling that he was about to try something. Mike had not informed the Escape Committee of his plans, nor indeed sought their approval, probably because the new conditions under which prisoners of war were now living might have led them to refuse consent for the attempt on the grounds that it was too dangerous.

The group heading for the park set off with Mike in it. Once there the guards took up their positions and the prisoners, as usual, began a game of football. Mike walked away by himself and was noticed by others in the park to be close to the fence pacing back and forth. After a few moments he took several steps back, removed his cloak to reveal civilian clothing underneath and a pair of large black gloves to protect his hands from the barbed wire, then ran at the perimeter fence. Stepping over the low warning wire Mike began to climb the wire fence and was immediately spotted by the guards who unslung their rifles to fire at him, but their *feldwebel* shouted: '*Nein, nicht schiessen, nicht schiessen!*' (No, don't fire, don't fire!).[3] Drawing his pistol as he went, the *feldwebel* ran round the fence and met Mike as he jumped down; 'It is no use Herr Sinclair,' he said. Rather than surrender Mike got to his feet, struck the pistol aside and sprinted off towards the cover of some trees about 150 yards away while at least three of the sentries, as well as a machine gunner positioned half-way up the slope towards the castle, opened fire. There was a stream that ran along a ravine on the western side of the open area beyond the park enclosure and then into a wood, it was this that Mike seemed to be heading towards, but it will never be known if he went in that direction expecting to reach open countryside beyond the trees or for some other reason. Lance Pope, who was in the park, saw what was happening and cried out '*Nicht schiessen! Nicht schiessen!*', but the shots continued. In all, twenty shots were fired at Mike – one of which found its target, ricocheting off his elbow, through both his lungs and into his heart, killing him instantly.

Gris, having returned to the room he shared with Mike after leaving him to walk down to the park alone, was sitting and writing a letter home. The room had a view toward the park, although trees and shrubs obscured it from direct sight. Hearing a fusillade of shots and shouting, he rushed to the window, convinced that the firing could only be associated with Mike. It was twenty minutes to four, as he later recorded in his diary. With a sense of foreboding, he went down to the courtyard as the walkers returned. Time passed slowly until, after what seemed an age, the gate opened. Seeing Lance Pope, Gris asked him what had happened.

"Mike Sinclair is dead," came the reply.

CHAPTER 15

LAID TO REST

On 28 September, three days after his death, the funeral for Mike took place in Colditz town cemetery. A party of officers, led by Hauptman Pűpcke followed by the SBO, Colonel Willy Tod, seven Officers and two Riflemen from the 60th, all on parole for the period of the burial, and lastly a *feldewebel* and twelve soldiers from the garrison left the castle to walk to the cemetery; the 60th contingent wore battledress with regimental badges of rank, black buttons and lanyards, everyone had boots and gaiters and all marched 'at ease'. The coffin was covered by a Union Jack with a 60th Officer's peaked cap lying on top; it was carried to the grave by the cemetery staff.

The service went very well in the circumstances, with Martin Gilliat reading John 14:1 – 'Let not your hearts be troubled; ye believe in God, believe also in me,' followed by the passage from *The Pilgrim's Progress* about Mr Valiant-for-Truth:

> Then said he, I am going to my Father's; and though with great difficulty I am got hither, yet now I do not repent me of all the trouble I have been at to arrive where I am. My sword I give to him that shall succeed me in my pilgrimage, and my courage and skill to him that can get it. My marks and scars I carry with me, to be a witness for me that I have fought His battles who now will be my rewarder.

> When the day that he must go hence was come, many accompanied him to the riverside, into which as he went he said, Death, where is thy sting? And as he went down deeper, he said, Grave, where is thy victory? So, he passed over, and all the trumpets sounded for him on the other side.

After lunch the same day there was a Memorial Service for Mike in the Colditz Chapel, ending with Last Post and Reveille, followed by the National Anthem. Reverend Richard (Dickie) Heard gave the address ending with:

> Finally, Mike was a believing Christian and one who'd known suffering and turned it to use. That's why although his death is a tragedy for his parents it isn't just a wasteful tragedy of a life. We say in our Creed that we believe in the resurrection of the Dead, and we know that Christ's promises are sure. Mike was the kind of man who wouldn't be confident about himself, but we who know him know that he is alright, and that he's met up with his younger brother who fell at Anzio, and the countless others who in their country's service have gone before us on the way that leads through death, but comes out in a brighter eternal world.

Later Martin Gilliat, Gris and Phil Pardoe carried out a 'Committee of Adjustment', a formal listing of the deceased's personal belongings before they are sent to the next of kin; when time and circumstances permit, letters and diary entries are read to ensure anything that might cause unnecessary distress is weeded out and retained separately. As the three carried out this task they found a note Mike had written and concealed in his belongings:

> I take full responsibility. Safe home to you,
> all you good chaps.

ANNEXES

Annex
A: Extract from *The Times*, Friday, 31 May 1940, reporting Admiral Somerville radio broadcast of 29 May 1940.

DEFENCE OF CALAIS

Magnificent Example of British Courage

Vice-Admiral Sir James Somerville broadcasting last night [29 May] and paying tribute to British courage and resolution said that he went over to Calais at night in one of our destroyers when the garrison was hard pressed, was surrounded by superior forces but was holding on grimly. As the destroyer made fast alongside the quay it came under heavy fire. With shells bursting alongside and on the quay the captain gave the order to cast off and with coolness and precision backed his ship clear of this unhealthy berth and brought her alongside at a spot which was less exposed to fire. Every order the captain gave was carried out faithfully and courageously regardless of the bursting shells.

On shore I found a Brigadier, a very gallant Brigadier, in command of our troops. He realised in full the situation in which he was placed and the need for maintaining the defence to the last minute. His quiet confidence, his grim determination to hold out to the last man was an inspiration to everyone there. No thought of surrender no thought but to serve their country to the utmost of their endeavour and to the last man. And this they did. The defence of Calais against overwhelming odds was a magnificent example of British courage.

Annex
B (i): Account of Second Lieutenant Peter Douglas escape and 'home run' with citation for MID

Peter Douglas was commissioned into the 8th Battalion Argyll & Sutherland Highlanders (TA) on 25 July 1939. A second date appears, 24 August 1939, which may relate to his mobilisation or a promotion to War Substantive Lieutenant. Further promotions, to W/S Captain on 26 November 1943 and to Temporary Major on 26 November 1943, are recorded. After the war he is shown as being on the Reserve of Officers with the rank of Hon. Major.

The *London Gazette* of 16 September 1941
The KING has been graciously pleased to approve that the following be mentioned in recognition of gallant and distinguished service in the field:

2nd Lt PFS Douglas DSO (93362) A&SH

A further entry in a supplement to the *London Gazette* of 16 March 1948 and published on the 19 March 1948, records the award by the King of Norway of the King Haakon VII Liberty Cross 'for distinguished service in the cause of the Allies'.

Annex
B (ii): CITATION FOR DISTINGUISHED SERVICE ORDER

Second-Lieutenant Peter Frederick (sic) Sholto Douglas (93562), Argyll and Sutherland Highlanders (Princess Louise's)

Second-Lieutenant Douglas escaped from Camp XXI D at Posen on 31st May 1941. As the camp was surrounded by a moat, and guarded by lights, wire and sentries, the only practicable means of escape was by means of the main gate. He therefore adopted a method which the officers in the camp had used before and with another officer was wheeled out on a trolley used to take out rubbish and emptied into the rubbish pit about fifty yards outside the camp. When the signal was given by accomplices watching on the roof they made their way south from the camp. Second-Lieutenant Douglas walked for eleven days until he reached a port. He was wearing civilian clothes the trousers being dyed battle dress and the coat tailored out of a summer blanket. When he reached Danzig he managed to evade a sentry and persuaded officials that he was a dock worker. Finally he stowed away on a Swedish steamer and arrived in Stockholm on 12 June 1941.

From MA Stockholm to MI9 – 16 June 1941

Report on escape Second Lieutenant Douglas

Escape had been attempted by tunnelling but proved impractical due to the water level. The only practical method of escape was by the main gate. Second Lieutenant Douglas adopted the same method of escape as had been used by four officers previously,[1] namely to get carried out of the main gate on the trolley used to take out rubbish and dustbin contents. After practice the officers became adept at folding themselves into a small space inside a sack with their head between their legs and learned to breathe without expanding or contracting the body and were thus able to avoid detection at the gate.

Douglas and a brother officer were conveyed out of the camp by two soldier accomplices and dumped into the rubbish pit about 50 yards from the camp. By a series of watchers on the fort roof they were given a signal when the coast was clear which did not occur for one hour as two of the guards were sunbathing. In the meantime, they were obliged to lie on some putrid fish awaiting the signal.

Douglas had civilian clothes the trousers of which were khaki battledress dyed in ink made up of four indelible pencils and ink. The coat he tailored himself of a summer blanket resembling cloth.

After leaving camp Douglas and his friend struck out south, i.e. away from the coast to avoid detection. They had only chocolate and malted milk tablets and Douglas walked for 11 days before boarding a goods train that carried him to Gdynia.

The name of the other officer was Cocksedge in the Royal Inniskilling Fusiliers. Douglas and Cocksedge separated as a result of being seen and chased at Ostrow approximately 80 miles southeast of Posen on the morning of the second day. Douglas does not know what happened to his friend, but he got clear and made his way to Danzig.

The docks were guarded but he got under the wire and dodged a sentry. He was stopped on the docks by two officials but he managed to give the impression that he was a dock worker who had left his pass at home and got away with it. He boarded a Swedish steamer and she sailed quite shortly after.

Douglas was kindly treated on board and landed in Sweden two days later.

Later in the war Peter Douglas joined the Special Operations Executive (SOE) and served in France behind German lines.

Account of escape from MI9 Interview 21 Jul 41

On 31 May, three days after the successful Littledale, Davies-Scourfield and Sinclair escape, the plan was repeated. Cooksedge and Douglas were put into sacks and carried out to the rubbish dump by orderlies but had to wait about an hour until receiving the 'all clear' signal enabling them to leave the rubbish pit. They made their way to Posen, but their contact did not appear and their attempts to find his house were unsuccessful. They therefore decided to make for Russia together.

Walking south they hit the railway going southeast and jumped a train hiding in the guard's compartment. The following morning, they arrived at Ostrow around 0100 where the train stopped and a civilian walked into their hiding place. They left as quickly as they could but since a number of people shouted after them, they split as they had planned to do in such circumstances and went different ways.

Douglas hid in the woods until dark when he walked due east hoping to find the railway line. The next day he decided to walk by day and on the fourth day took the decision to head for Sweden. As his food had run out he approached farmhouses to ask for water and was often given food; he also got information on the direction to travel. On the tenth day he reached the railway; some Poles living alongside the line, although frightened, sheltered him for two days providing food and water.

He boarded a train and travelled in a coal truck to Danzig leaving the train outside the town in the dock area. He spotted a hole in the wire and was able to reach the quay where he was approached by a German official asking him to do some work. He was taken to another official who asked for his work ticket and dismissed him when he could not produce one. He stayed in the dock area and made his way to an area of cranes, between which and the ships, was not visited by the officials and was comparatively safe. He walked on board a Swedish ship, SS Polcirkeln, and was able to make contact with a Swede who agreed to turn his back while Douglas stowed away. The following day he was officially discovered by the mate and taken to the captain who agreed to let Douglas remain on board until the ship docked in Sweden. The following morning on docking at Oxelosund he was put in goal for two days before being collected by the (British) Consul.

Annex
C: Proof of Evidence of Lieutenant AM Sinclair KRRC

On the night in question, shortly before the incident complained of, I was engaged in an attempt to escape, dressed in clothes resembling German uniform. It was vital to the execution of the plan of escape that I should relieve the German sentry number 3 of his post and hand the post over to one of the British Officers dressed as a German soldier. At first sentry number 5 seemed willing to hand over his post but then thought better of it and shouted to sentry number 6 to sound the alarm and told me to stay where I was. Sentry number 5 covered me with his rifle and soon after *Obergefreiter* Pilz appeared on the scene and covered Hyde-Thomson with his revolver.

Shortly after two parties of Germans appeared on the scene, one from the left and one from the right. An under-officer whom I can easily recognise and who shouted in a high squeaky voice was in charge of the second group from the right. His whole attitude was one to provoke and increase the tension and excitement instead of taking charge. He drew his pistol and brandished it in a reckless and gleeful manner and obviously was enjoying the chance of having a possibility of using it. In my opinion his behaviour greatly contributed to the tension and excitement which led to the firing of the shot. He screamed at me 'Hands up!' and I shouted back 'My hands are up they are high enough,' then he repeatedly shouted at me a word which sounded like 'abschnallen', to which I replied that I didn't understand [*abschnallen* means disarm yourself].

Owing to the state of confusion, I do not remember exactly when the next incident, namely the shot, took place, but I do remember being extremely surprised that a shot should be fired for I was well within the wired perimeter of the camp at a spot which was well lighted by the arc lamps, and was standing with my hands raised above my head in a gesture of obvious surrender; and there was no cause whatever for a shot to be fired.

The shot came from in front of me, and a foot to the left while I was still facing the underofficer in charge of the second party; *Obergefreiter* Pilz fired the shot. When I was hit, I sank to my knees. Eventually we were told to move off and I was expected to move without any help. I replied in German, 'how can I when I have been shot through the chest?' (Annex D); no German made any attempt to help me in any manner whatsoever. I was not carrying any firearms. I had a dummy wooden pistol in my pocket which I did not produce, and which was first discovered and removed from my pocket by a German officer long after the shooting when I had been put into the cells instead of the sick-bay.'

Signed
A.M. Sinclair, Lt KRRC
13th March 1944

Annex
D: Obituary Miss Jane Walker – aka Mrs Markowska

The Times 1963 Colonel EGB Davies-Scourfield writes

The death of Miss Jane Walker MBE on November 12 in a Bexhill nursing home should not be allowed to pass unnoticed.

Originally a governess to the Royal Family of the Austro-Hungarian Empire she married a Pole and in 1920 settled with him in Warsaw. In 1945 she managed to escape to England and thereafter assumed her maiden name.

An intense and almost overbearing patriot she had a knack of becoming embroiled in political upheavals. Many who knew her in Bexhill during her declining years would have been surprised to know that her life had been packed with adventure and danger and that in turn she had been on the 'wanted list' either for espionage, sabotage or political 'crimes' by the Austro-Hungarian police, the revolutionaries of Bela-Kun, Hitler's Gestapo and finally Stalin's secret police.

In both World Wars she devoted her energy and courage to helping escaped British prisoners of war, and many today owe her their lives. By 1942 she had built quite a considerable organisation in Warsaw and was supported by the Polish Resistance Movement. Gradually the Gestapo learnt of her activities, but she succeeded in evading arrest and was eventually forced to leave Warsaw and hide as a peasant in the country. There she later became embroiled in the Russian advance towards the Vistula and finally, after many further adventures, managed to reach the British Military Mission at Odessa dressed, curiously enough, as an NCO in the RAF.

She was a great patriot of the old-fashioned kind, breathing with her every breath fire, slaughter and defiance of Britain's enemies. She was tyrannical, obstinate and intolerant; she was also capable of great affection, sympathy and unselfishness, and in war to risk her life was all part of the day's work if it was for her country, fellow countrymen or their allies.

Old age has now worn her down at last. But she lives in the memories of all who knew her and loved her in dark and dangerous days.

NOTES

Chapter 2

1. Extract from 'Blitzkrieg in their Own Words', a translation of 'Mit den Panzern in Ost und West' published in Germany in 1942 with a Foreword by Generaloberst Heinz Guderian
2. 'From Calais to Colditz', Philip Pardoe. Pen and Sword 2015 page 45

Chapter 3

1. 'From Calais to Colditz', Philip Pardoe. Pen and Sword 2015 page 71.
2. 'From Calais to Colditz', Philip Pardoe. Pen and Sword page 72.

Chapter 4

1. Convention relative to the Treatment of Prisoners of War. Geneva, 27 July 1929. Chapter 3 'Hygiene in Camps', Article 13
2. Pat Reid was to write a number of books in the 1950s and later that caught the imagination of the public. These were largely responsible for the interest taken in Colditz and those imprisoned there.

Chapter 5

1. Peter Douglas, A&SH, was to assist in a later successful escape by Mike, Ronnie and Gris. He himself escaped later and made a 'home run'; his story is covered in Annex A to Chapter 5.
2. If compasses were not available they were improvised by stroking the length of darning needles with a small magnet for several hours until sufficiently magnetised to mount on a small circular card with a luminous watch hour hand stuck on to point north. These could then be mounted in a round aluminium tin from which the top was cut and replaced with talc. While not very accurate they gave the general direction and retained their magnetism for several weeks.

Chapter 6

1. The 'all clear' signal was given by Peter Douglas who later used the same method to escape from Fort VIII and made a home run after stowing away on a Swedish vessel in Danzig as is covered in Annex B.

Chapter 7

1. Mrs M was an English lady who assisted British POWs to escape to England in both World Wars. She was on the Soviet Union 'wanted list' in 1945 at the end of WW2 but managed to evade arrest and flee to England herself. She died in 1963 in Bexhill on Sea, Sussex; her Obituary in The Times written by Gris Davies-Scourfield is at Annexe A.
2. One individual she had helped was Rifleman D Hosington, 2KRRC. He had been captured at Calais and escaped in October 1940 from Stalag XX1B. He made a home run via Greece for which achievement he was awarded the DCM.
3. Mr Olszewski known as 'Puffy' was the founder with Mrs Markowski of the underground movement to assist British escaped POWs in Warsaw. His flat was under surveillance by Gestapo

investigating the suspected escape organisation and he was arrested when he returned there. Sent to Auschwitz he survived many months there before being moved to Sachenhausen concentration camp where he died or was killed, it is not known which.

4. SS stood for the 'Schutzstaffel' (Protective Echelon). Formed as Hitler's personal bodyguards, they became one of the most powerful and feared organisations in Nazi Germany headed up by Himmler; recruits had to prove that none of their ancestors *were Jewish* and were taught they were elite troops. There were two main constituent groups, the Allgemeine SS (General SS) responsible for enforcing the racial policy of Nazi Germany and general policing and the Waffen-SS (Armed SS) that consisted of combat units embedded in Germany's army. A third component, the SS-Totenkopfverb.nde, Death's Head Units, ran. the concentration and extermination camps.

Chapter 8

1. Heydrich died from his injuries eight days later.

Chapter 9

1. But through ingenious tunnelling and various ruses individuals managed to get out of the castle and the surrounding grounds on 130 occasions. A total of 32 escapees succeeded in reaching the frontier of a neutral state and freedom before the Castle was liberated by American forces on 16 April 1945.
2. 'Calais to Colditz', Philip Pardoe. Pen and Sword 2015, page 124

Chapter 10

1. 'They Have Their Exits', Airey Neave, Pen and Sword reprint 2013, page 64.
2. Julius Green was Jewish and a dentist in Edinburgh. He joined the TA at the start of WW2 and was captured in June 1940

when France fell. He spent many months travelling between POW camps providing dental work for POWs and German troops, hiding his Judaism by disposing of his identity discs and claiming to be a Presbyterian; he was helped by a Medical Officer asserting that he had been circumcised for medical reasons. Shortly after his capture he was recruited by MI9 to relay information from POW camps; he wrote coded letters to his family and friends which would then be analysed by them providing information on German troop movements and railway lines, what troops should bring with them if captured and what should be sent to Colditz to help POWs escape efforts.

3. 'Colditz The German Story' Rheinhold Eggers, Robert Hale Ltd 1961, page 28.

Chapter 11

1. Extract from Charles Klein letter to the author.
2. Extract from Charles Klein letter to the author..

Chapter 12

1. The rifles used by the German guards were French. The wooden replica weapons for the escape were produced using a home made lathe. Advice on their look and authenticity was given by French prisoners

Chapter 13

1. Jack Best was captured In 1941 after ditching in the Mediterranean on patrol out of Malta. Sent to a series of German prison camps in June 1942 he and two others tunnelled out

beyond the perimeter wire, and walked into the nearby woods. They planned to steal a Junkers transport plane and fly out of Germany but, after observing several airfields, they abandoned the scheme in favour of stowing away on a Sweden-bound ship at Stettin (Czezecin). Surviving on raw potatoes, they reached the river Oder, but were discovered asleep under a skiff and sent to Colditz.

2. After his recapture and return to Colditz he sent an SOS for naval buttons, needle and cotton and was able to reconvert the uniform and return it to its owner.
3. See page 112.

Chapter 14

1. Of the 76 who got out 73 were recaptured. Of these 51 were executed, 17 were returned to Stalag Luft III, 2 were sent to Colditz and 4 to Sachsenhausen concentration camp
2. Lockwood had been captured retreating to Dunkirk in May 1940 and sent to Laufen from where he escaped but was recaptured and sent to Colditz Castle as one of six British prisoners to join three Canadians and over one hundred Poles already there. He made several attempts to escape but never succeeded in making a home run himself and was still at the castle acting as 'Treasurer' of the Escape Committee when it was liberated by the US Army.
3. The Feldewebel who was supervising the walk was normally in charge of the town cells and regarded as a decent man by the Officer prisoners. He knew and greatly admired Mike, hence in all probability his wish to stop what he perceived to be an escape that was already compromised and doomed to fail.

ACKNOWLEDGEMENTS

Many thanks to all involved in bringing Mike's story to life in this book.

Particular thanks to Paul Harris for his support editing.

Thank you to Penny, my wife, for fifty years of companionship, support and patience as a military wife and during the hours I spent in my study getting this story down. And to my four girls for your support and unofficial IT consultancy!